THE YEAR IN
BEER
2017
diary

CAMPAIGN
FOR
REAL ALE

BOOKS

Published by the Campaign for Real Ale Ltd.
230 Hatfield Road
St Albans
Hertfordshire AL1 4LW

www.camra.org.uk/books

Design and layout © Campaign for Real Ale Ltd. 2016

Text on pages 3, 8, 10–11, 12–116, 124–125 © Jeff Evans
and taken from *A Beer a Day* (first published 2008)
and CAMRA's *Book of Beer Knowledge* – 2nd edition
(first published 2011), both original works by Jeff Evans
and published by CAMRA Books.

The right of Jeff Evans to be identified as the
author of the text as detailed above has been
asserted by him in accordance with the Copyright,
Designs and Patents Act 1988

All other text © Campaign for Real Ale Ltd. 2016

ISBN 978-1-85249-337-0

A CIP catalogue record for this book is available
from the British Library

Printed and bound in China by Latitude Press Ltd

Head of Publishing: Simon Hall
Project Editor: Katie Button
Editorial Assistance: Susannah Lord, Julie Hudson
Design/Typography: Dale Tomlinson
Sales & Marketing: David Birkett

Moon phases

● New moon
◐ First quarter
○ Full moon
◑ Third quarter

Picture credits

The Publisher would like to thank all those
who have kindly given permission for their
photography to be reproduced in this guide.
Specific thanks go to:

Cover: Piotr Zajc/Shutterstock;
p14 Sophotographie/Alamy Stock Photo;
p16 Simon Price/Alamy Stock Photo;
p18 Chris Howes/Wild Places Photography/
Alamy Stock Photo; p22 Glasshouse Images/
Alamy Stock Photo; p24 Zoonar GmbH/
Alamy Stock Photo; p28 Neale Haynes/
REX/Shutterstock; p30 Marco Verch/flickr;
p32 (top) Joe Stange; p32 (bottom) OPT –
JL Flémal/www.visitbelgium.com; p36 Loop
Images Ltd/Alamy Stock Photo; p38 REX/
Shutterstock; p46 Chris Phutully/flickr;
p50 Military Images/Alamy Stock Photo;
p52 Classic Image/Alamy Stock Photo;
p54 North Wind Picture Archives/Alamy
Stock Photo; p58 Ute Grabowsky/photothek
images UG/Alamy Stock Photo; p60 Radharc
Images/Alamy Stock Photo; p62 Galaxy
Picture Library/Alamy Stock Photo; p64
Thank you for visiting my page/flickr; p66
Isle of Man/Alamy Stock Photo; p68 Hemis/
Alamy Stock Photo; p70 Archive Image/
Alamy Stock Photo; p72 Art Directors &
TRIP/Alamy Stock Photo; p74 Gavin Rodgers/
Alamy Stock Photo; p76 Vassilis/flickr; p80
South West Images Scotland/Alamy Stock
Photo; p82 Maurice Crooks/Alamy Stock
Photo; p84 Adrian Sherratt/Alamy Stock
Photo; p88 Katie Button; p92 Navin75/flickr;
p94 Dennis Jarvis/flickr; p98 IanDagnall
Computing/Alamy Stock Photo; p100
StockyStock/Alamy Stock Photo; p102
(top) Trinity Mirror/Mirrorpix/Alamy Stock
Photo; p102 (bottom) Smörgåsbord; p104
MARKA/Alamy Stock Photo; p112 IanDagnall
Computing/Alamy Stock Photo; p116 World
History Archive/Alamy Stock Photo.

A diary with a difference

WELCOME to a diary with a difference. *The Year in Beer* is a celebration of high days, holidays and the passing of the seasons as seen through the eyes of the world's greatest brewers. Major anniversaries, religious feasts and important birthdays come under the spotlight, along with commemorations, carnivals and some even more eccentric events. Whatever the occasion, there is always a beer for it, and there is no more fitting beverage with which to toast the unfolding of each day, week and month.

Beer has always danced to the tune of the seasons. In pre-industrial times, brewing in summer months in many parts of the world was impossible, due to the difficulty of controlling fermentation. Hence, brewers took to brewing beers in the winter that could be kept for enjoyment later. This is the origin of harvest ales in Britain, *bières de garde* in France, *saisons* in Belgium and of *Märzen* beers in Germany. It's also a major part of the story of lager: it was while needing to store beer for a long period in cold conditions to keep it fresh that monks discovered the benefits of lagering.

Today, there is a new seasonality to brewing. For drinkers clamouring for new and tempting beers, breweries have re-introduced the concept of seasonals, so you'll find spring, summer and autumn ales to join the winter offering. Specials are also brewed to celebrate events such as St Valentine's Day, Easter, May Day, Halloween and Bonfire Night.

The Year in Beer selects some of the most interesting new seasonals and brings them together with other beers that do a terrific job in keeping alive the memories of historic events and great achievers. Looking for once behind the pump clips and labels, it unearths fine beers that vibrantly recall glorious and sometimes inglorious moments of history, beers that mark cultural highlights, and beers that have been inspired by religion and culture. This is not just a diary, this is a beer almanac, with a story for every beer and a beer for every story.

Personal information

Name

Address

Postcode

Email

Phone (home)

Phone (work)

Mobile

Other details

Public holidays and observances 2017

JANUARY
1 New Year's Day; Last day of Hanukkah
2 **Public holiday UK**
3 **Public holiday Scotland**
6 Epiphany
25 Burn's Night
28 Chinese New Year

FEBRUARY
14 Valentine's Day
28 Shrove Tuesday

MARCH
1 St. David's Day; Ash Wednesday
12 Purim
17 St Patrick's Day;
   Public holiday Northern Ireland
20 Spring equinox
26 Daylight Saving Time starts;
   Mothering Sunday

APRIL
9 Palm Sunday
11 First day of Passover
14 Good Friday; **Public holiday UK**
17 Easter Monday; **Public holiday England,
   Wales & Northern Ireland**
18 Last day of Passover
23 St George's Day

MAY
1 Beltane; **Public holiday UK**
27 Ramadan begins
29 **Public holiday UK**

JUNE
18 Father's Day
21 Summer solstice
26 Eid-al-Fitr

JULY
12 Battle of the Boyne;
   Public holiday Northern Ireland

AUGUST
7 **Public holiday Scotland**
28 **Public holiday England,
   Wales & Northern Ireland**

SEPTEMBER
2 Eid-al-Adha
21 Rosh Hashana
22 Autumn Equinox; Islamic New Year
30 Yom Kippur

OCTOBER
19 Diwali
29 Daylight Saving Time ends
31 Halloween

NOVEMBER
1 All Saint' Day
2 All Souls' Day
5 Guy Fawkes Day
11 Remembrance Day
12 Remembrance Sunday
30 St Andrew's Day;
   Public holiday Scotland

DECEMBER
1 Prophet's Birthday
3 First Sunday of Advent
13 First Day of Hanukkah
20 Last day of Hanukkah
21 Winter solstice
24 Christmas Eve
25 Christmas Day; **Public holiday UK**
26 Boxing Day; **Public holiday UK**
31 New Year's Eve

2017 calendar

JANUARY

Monday		2	9	16	23	30
Tuesday		3	10	17	24	31
Wednesday		4	11	18	25	
Thursday		5	12	19	26	
Friday		6	13	20	27	
Saturday		7	14	21	28	
Sunday	1	8	15	22	29	

FEBRUARY

Monday		6	13	20	27
Tuesday		7	14	21	28
Wednesday	1	8	15	22	
Thursday	2	9	16	23	
Friday	3	10	17	24	
Saturday	4	11	18	25	
Sunday	5	12	19	26	

MARCH

Monday		6	13	20	27
Tuesday		7	14	21	28
Wednesday	1	8	15	22	29
Thursday	2	9	16	23	30
Friday	3	10	17	24	31
Saturday	4	11	18	25	
Sunday	5	12	19	26	

APRIL

Monday		3	10	17	24
Tuesday		4	11	18	25
Wednesday		5	12	19	26
Thursday		6	13	20	27
Friday		7	14	21	28
Saturday	1	8	15	22	29
Sunday	2	9	16	23	30

MAY

Monday	1	8	15	22	29
Tuesday	2	9	16	23	30
Wednesday	3	10	17	24	31
Thursday	4	11	18	25	
Friday	5	12	19	26	
Saturday	6	13	20	27	
Sunday	7	14	21	28	

JUNE

Monday		5	12	19	26
Tuesday		6	13	20	27
Wednesday		7	14	21	28
Thursday	1	8	15	22	29
Friday	2	9	16	23	30
Saturday	3	10	17	24	
Sunday	4	11	18	25	

JULY

Monday		3	10	17	24	31
Tuesday		4	11	18	25	
Wednesday		5	12	19	26	
Thursday		6	13	20	27	
Friday		7	14	21	28	
Saturday	1	8	15	22	29	
Sunday	2	9	16	23	30	

AUGUST

Monday		7	14	21	28
Tuesday	1	8	15	22	29
Wednesday	2	9	16	23	30
Thursday	3	10	17	24	31
Friday	4	11	18	25	
Saturday	5	12	19	26	
Sunday	6	13	20	27	

SEPTEMBER

Monday		4	11	18	25
Tuesday		5	12	19	26
Wednesday		6	13	20	27
Thursday		7	14	21	28
Friday	1	8	15	22	29
Saturday	2	9	16	23	30
Sunday	3	10	17	24	

OCTOBER

Monday	2	9	16	23	30
Tuesday	3	10	17	24	31
Wednesday	4	11	18	25	
Thursday	5	12	19	26	
Friday	6	13	20	27	
Saturday	7	14	21	28	
Sunday	1	8	15	22	29

NOVEMBER

Monday		6	13	20	27
Tuesday		7	14	21	28
Wednesday	1	8	15	22	29
Thursday	2	9	16	23	30
Friday	3	10	17	24	
Saturday	4	11	18	25	
Sunday	5	12	19	26	

DECEMBER

Monday		4	11	18	25
Tuesday		5	12	19	26
Wednesday		6	13	20	27
Thursday		7	14	21	28
Friday	1	8	15	22	29
Saturday	2	9	16	23	30
Sunday	3	10	17	24	31

Beer's patron saints' days

Beer enjoys the patronage of numerous saints, some only because of rather limited associations with beer and brewers, but others because they were said to have performed miracles and other feats involving beer. Listed below are the most prominent and their beery connections.

31 January
St Veronus (?–863). Miracle worker adopted by the lambic brewers of the Payottenland region, near Brussels, Belgium.

1 February
St Brigid/Bridget of Ireland (453–523). Pious chieftain's daughter (possibly) who turned her bathwater into beer to serve a visiting cleric.

18 July
St Arnold/Arnulf of Metz (580–640). Bishop of Metz whose funeral pallbearers were refreshed by a bottomless mug of beer.

10 August
St Lawrence (?–258). Papal deacon roasted alive by anti-Christian Emperor Valerian; brewers sought his patronage because they also often suffered fiery deaths in ancient times.

14 August
St Arnold/Arnulf of Soissons (1040–1087). Bishop of Soissons who advised his flock to drink beer rather than water, as it was safer.

28 August
St Augustine of Hippo (354–430). Bishop of Hippo (Algeria) who formerly enjoyed a hedonistic lifestyle, including copious beer drinking.

17 September
St Hildegarde of Bingen (1098–1179). Benedictine abbess and polymath who promoted the use of hops in beer.

21 November
St Columbanus (543–615). Irish itinerant missionary who multiplied bread and beer to feed his followers.

CAMRA's beer festivals in 2017

The Campaign for Real Ale's beer festivals showcase cask beer in all its glory and underscore the brilliant choice now available to beer lovers. They are staffed by CAMRA volunteers and are vital shop windows for independent breweries and often feature great beers from around the country that may be hard-to-find in the area where festivals are based. Some festivals specialise in particular styles, such as winter beers, and most offer cider and perry, along with food, live music and family facilities. CAMRA runs over 200 festivals a year, below are those festivals whose dates are confirmed for 2017. For more details about CAMRA festivals check www.camra.org.uk/events

January

19–21	Cambridge Winter Ale Festival
19–21	Manchester Beer & Cider Festival
27–28	Salisbury Winterfest, Wiltshire

February

2–4	Tewkesbury Winter Ales Festival
9–11	Fleetwood Beer Festival
10–12	Hucknall Beer Festival
15–18	Chelmsford Winter Beer & Cider Festival, Essex
16–18	Luton Beer & Cider Festival
17–18	**National Winter Ales Festival**, Norwich

March

16–18	Leeds Beer, Cider & Perry Festival
17–18	Wantage Beer Festival, Oxfordshire
17–18	Winchester Real Ale & Cider Festival
23–25	Bristol Beer Festival
31–1 *April*	Chippenham Beer Festival, Wiltshire
31–1 *April*	Oldham Beer Festival, Greater Manchester

April

7–9	**CAMRA Members' Weekend**, Bournemouth
14–15	Planet Thanet Easter Beer Festival, Margate
19–22	East Anglian Beer & Cider Festival, Bury St Edmunds, Suffolk
26–29	Newcastle Beer & Cider Festival, Tyne & Wear
27–29	Farnham Beer Festival, Surrey
27–29	Hull Real Ale & Cider Festival

May

22–27	Cambridge Beer Festival

June

1–3	Stockport Beer & Cider Festival, Greater Manchester
16–17	Salisbury Beerex, Wiltshire

July

4–8	Chelmsford Summer Beer & Cider Festival, Essex
6–8	Scottish Real Ale Festival, Edinburgh
7–9	Beer on the Wye, Hereford
20–22	Kent Beer Festival, Canterbury

August

3–5	Worcester Beer, Cider & Perry Festival
8–12	**Great British Beer Festival**, Olympia, London
22–26	Peterborough Beer Festival

September

5–9	Chappel Beer Festival, Essex
14–17	York Beer & Cider Festival
27–30	St Albans Beer & Cider Festival

October

6–7	Ascot Beer Festival, Berkshire
11–14	Robin Hood Beer Festival, Nottingham
27–28	Poole Beer Festival, Dorset

December

5–9	Pigs Ear Beer & Cider Festival, Hackney, London

Sizes, shapes and conversions

Barrels, casks and kegs

When your bartender says he's just off to 'change the barrel', it's extremely unlikely that he'll be doing exactly that. A barrel is actually an imperial measure of 36 gallons (approximately 164 litres) and, such is the demand for greater choice and faster turnover of beers, very few barrels are rolled out into the pub trade these days. The proper term for a real ale container is a cask (hence the term 'cask-conditioned ale'), and casks are now generally limited to 18-gallon (kilderkin) and 9-gallon (firkin) sizes (see full list of cask sizes below). A keg is a different kind of beer container, devised for holding and dispensing pressurized beer. A commonly used keg size is 11 gallons (approximately 50 litres).

Traditional cask sizes

Butt	108 gallons (*no longer used*)
Puncheon	72 gallons (*no longer used*)
Hogshead	54 gallons (*now rarely used*)
Barrel	36 gallons
Half Hogshead	27 gallons (*now rarely used*)
Kilderkin or Kil/Kiln	18 gallons
Anker	10 gallons (*now rarely used*)
Firkin	9 gallons
Pin	4½ gallons

Some popular beer glass shapes

Shaker
Used for ales, particularly in the USA. Originally devised as part of the kit for 'shaking' and serving cocktails.

Tulip
Used for ales, particularly in the UK. A shapely, more aesthetically pleasing version of the straight 'sleeve' pint glass.

Nonic
Used for ales, particularly in the UK. The bulge is intended to prevent the rims chipping in the glass washer (hence 'no nick').

Weissbier Glass
Used for German-style wheat beers. The extended height and tapering shape allow the thick foam to be captured at the top.

Chalice or Goblet
Used for strong ales, particularly in Belgium. The shape and name echo the religious origins of Trappist and Abbey beers.

Pilsner Glass
Used for true pilsner lagers, particularly in Germany. The tapered shape allows deep foam to collect at the top.

Stemmed Tulip
Used for strong ales, particularly in Belgium. The curved shape both retains foam and allows aromas to be accentuated.

Seidel
Used for helles and other lagers, particularly in Germany. The thick glass and handle help to keep the beer cold.

Imperial and metric conversion formulae

From	To	Multiply by
Pints	litres	0.5683
litres	pints	1.7597
Gallons	litres	4.5461
litres	gallons	0.22
Gallons	hectolitres	0.0455
hectolitres	gallons	21.997
Barrels	hectolitres	1.6366
hectolitres	barrels	0.611

From	To	Multiply by
inches	centimetres	2.54
centimetres	inches	0.3937
feet	metres	0.3048
metres	feet	3.281
yards	metres	0.9144
metres	yards	1.094
miles	kilometres	1.609
kilometres	miles	0.6214

From	To	Multiply by
ounces	grams	28.35
grams	ounces	0.0352
pounds	grams	453.6
grams	pounds	0.0022
pounds	kilograms	0.4536
kilograms	pounds	2.205
tons	kilograms	1016
kilograms	tons	0.0009

Imperial beer measurements

Barrel	36 gallons
Gallon	8 pints
Quart	2 pints (40 fluid ounces)
Pint	20 fluid ounces
Nip	⅓ pint
Gill	5 fluid ounces (¼ pint)
Yard of Ale	2¼ – 4½ pints (not standard)

US beer measurements

Barrel	31 gallons
Gallon	8 pints
Quart	2 pints (32 fluid ounces)
Pint	16 fluid ounces

Recommended beer serving temperatures

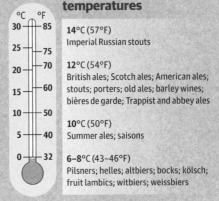

14°C (57°F)
Imperial Russian stouts

12°C (54°F)
British ales; Scotch ales; American ales; stouts; porters; old ales; barley wines; bières de garde; Trappist and abbey ales

10°C (50°F)
Summer ales; saisons

6–8°C (43–46°F)
Pilsners; helles; altbiers; bocks; kölsch; fruit lambics; witbiers; weissbiers

Temperature conversion formulae

°F to °C: Deduct 32, then multiply by 5, then divide by 9
°C to °F: Multiply by 9, then divide by 5, then add 32

Units of alcohol

A unit is a measure of 10 ml of pure alcohol. In the UK, these units are increasingly being shown on containers. However, where this is not the case, for example when you buy a pint of beer in a pub, you can work out how many units are in it for yourself, using the following formula:

Volume in millilitres (ml) × % alcohol by volume (ABV) then divide by 1000

A pint is equivalent to 568 ml. So to find the units in a pint of beer at 3.5% ABV, multiply 568 × 3.5, then divide by 1000 = 1.988 units. A pint of beer at 5% ABV is 568 × 5 divided by 1000 = 2.84 units. Note, however that other countries have different values for units.

Weihenstephaner Pilsner (5.1%)

Source Bavarian State Brewery, Freising

brauerei-weihenstephan.de

26th December – St Stephen's Day

The feast of Stephen, or St Stephen's Day, is rarely mentioned these days, overshadowed by the British holiday Boxing Day that is celebrated on the same date. St Stephen was one of the early deacons of the Christian church, charged with the distribution of alms to the needy. He was born a Jew, and he paid the price for his religious conversion by being stoned to death by those with whom he had once joined in prayer. Thus Stephen became the first Christian martyr.

Weihenstephan, based in Freising, just north of Munich, claims to be the oldest brewery in the world, dating from the year 1040. It started out as an abbey in the eighth century. More importantly, for today, the name Weihenstephan translates as 'Holy Stephen' after the hill named after the saint on which the brewery stands.

Weihenstephan is rare in being owned by the Bavarian state. Its speciality is weissbier, but it also turns out some other fine beers, including a pilsner that would make a fine palate sharpener before a Boxing Day lunch of cold meats and pickles. Pale golden in colour, this clean, crisp beer has a surprisingly fruity aroma – suggestions of melon, peach and pear to me. Tastewise, it's fairly sweet for this style of beer but, as you'd expect, does have an overlay of firm, tangy Hallertauer hops, which continue through into the long, drying, herbal finish. The brewery describes its pilsner as 'a cut above the ordinary', and that's certainly something beer connoisseurs are looking for at this time of the year.

26 Monday
Boxing Day
Public holiday UK

27 Tuesday
Public holiday UK

28 Wednesday

29 Thursday ●

30 Friday

31 Saturday
New Year's Eve

1 Sunday
New Year's Day, Last day of Hanukkah

Monday	26	2	9	16	23	30
Tuesday	27	3	10	17	24	31
Wednesday	28	4	11	18	25	
Thursday	29	5	12	19	26	
Friday	30	6	13	20	27	
Saturday	31	7	14	21	28	
Sunday	1	8	15	22	29	

Harvey's Imperial Extra Double Stout (9%)

Harvey & Son, Lewes, East Sussex

harveysonline.co.uk

7th January – Russian Orthodox Christmas

If you haven't indulged enough over the Christmas and New Year holidays, you can extend your celebrations by a week by marking the Russian Orthodox Christmas on 7 January (the Russian Orthodox Church still uses the Julian calendar, which is 13 days behind that used in the West).

Russians have revived their Christmas celebrations since the downfall of the Soviet Union and the collapse of Communist control. The festivities begin with a 12-course vegetarian feast on Christmas Eve (marking the end of a fasting period) and include gifts for children delivered by Grandfather Frost, a Santa Claus figure who is accompanied by his granddaughter, named Snowmaiden.

Given the traditional fondness for strong dark stouts in this part of the world, it would seem highly appropriate to mark the occasion with a glass or two of an Imperial Russian Stout. These rich, malty yet well-hopped beers were once shipped regularly from Britain across the icy Baltic to warm the cockles of Russian aristocrats, particularly those in the court of Empress Catherine the Great. Possibly the most authentic recreation of the style comes from Harvey's in Sussex. Their Imperial Extra Double Stout is a beer with muscle, thick and strong, malty and vinous, with a coffeeish finish. It's surprisingly mellow, once you get the hang of it, but it's definitely one for special occasions rather than everyday drinking. A Russian Christmas would fit the bill.

Saint Basil's Cathedral, Moscow at Christmas

2 Monday
Public holiday UK

3 Tuesday
Public holiday Scotland

4 Wednesday

5 Thursday ☽

6 Friday
Epiphany

7 Saturday

8 Sunday

Monday		2	9	16	23	30
Tuesday		3	10	17	24	31
Wednesday		4	11	18	25	
Thursday		5	12	19	26	
Friday		6	13	20	27	
Saturday		7	14	21	28	
Sunday	1	8	15	22	29	

Innis & Gunn Oak-Aged Beer (6.6%)

Innis & Gunn Brewing Co, Inveralmond, Perth

innisandgunn.com

11th January – Burning of the Clavie

There are few more arcane rituals than the Burning of the Clavie, which takes place every 11 January at Burghead, near Elgin, Scotland. The ceremony involves carrying a lit half-barrel filled with wood and tar through town, with smouldering embers offered to selected households for luck.

The origins of the festival are disputed. Some say it was Roman; others place the ritual in Pictish or Norse traditions. The barrel used at one time would have been rescued from the fishing industry, but these days it is usually a whisky cask.

Whisky casks also do a fine job of creating one of Scotland's most interesting beers. It is said that Innis & Gunn's Oak Aged Beer was discovered by accident. Caledonian Brewery executive Dougal Sharp was commissioned by a whisky distiller to brew a beer to provide a beer 'finish' to one of its whiskies. (It is common for whiskies to have port or sherry finishes, created by filling oak casks with fortified wine so that the wood absorbs the flavour and then passes it on to whisky when the cask is refilled.) Dougal's beer was mostly thrown away once it had served its purpose but some canny workers realized that the beer was not just drinkable, but also rather special, having acquired vanilla, toffee and citrus notes from the wood.

When told about this, Dougal set up Innis & Gunn to exploit the idea. He now has beer brewed under contract at an unnamed Scottish brewery. This is aged for 30 days in white oak casks originally intended for the Bourbon industry and is then blended with that from other oak casks in a marrying tun, where it sits for 47 days. The vanilla and toffee notes certainly show through in both aroma and taste, along with gentle hints of lemon, before a warming, oaky finish. It would be just the job after a chilly January ramble around a fishing town in the north of Scotland.

A burning 'clavie' being marched through Burghead

9 Monday

13 Friday

10 Tuesday

14 Saturday

11 Wednesday

15 Sunday

12 Thursday ○

Monday		2	9	16	23	30
Tuesday		3	10	17	24	31
Wednesday		4	11	18	25	
Thursday		5	12	19	26	
Friday		6	13	20	27	
Saturday		7	14	21	28	
Sunday	1	8	15	22	29	

Arkell's Bee's Organic Ale (4.5%)

Arkell's Brewery Ltd, Swindon, Wiltshire

arkells.com

AA Milne's ever-popular *Winnie the Pooh* books

18th January – Winnie the Pooh Day

18 January 1882 was the birthday of Alan Alexander (AA) Milne, and some grateful person, identity unknown, has declared this day to be Winnie the Pooh Day. The misadventures of Winnie the Pooh, Christopher Robin, Piglet, Eeyore, Tigger and others have captivated children since the 1920s. Milne based his tales on the nursery toys played with by his son, Christopher Robin Milne, and set the action in the Hundred Acre Wood, inspired by Ashdown Forest in Sussex, where Milne and his family lived.

If Pooh has one obsession it is with getting some honey. One of his best-known mishaps comes about when he uses a party balloon to fly close to a bees' nest in the hope of stealing their honey. Like most Pooh tales, it ends uncomfortably, with the bees seeking revenge.

Honey when used in brewing adds a mellow softness, which is particularly noticeable on the swallow. Bee's Organic Ale, from Arkell's Brewery in Swindon boasts on the label that it is made with real honey. Pale malt is joined by a little crystal malt and some wheat malt in the mash tun; the hops in the copper are First Gold, with Hallertauer from New Zealand added as the beer is strained through the hop back. The honey also goes in the copper. The result is a golden beer with a fresh and appealing aroma – spicy, malty, honeyed and floral, with suggestions of pineapple. On the palate, the beer is soft and velvety. The honey is obvious but doesn't destroy the balance, which falls just on the bitter side of bittersweet, with floral and pineapple notes floating around. Honeyed malt lingers after the swallow until bitter hops eventually take over, but this is a mellow finish, with no sting in the tail.

16 Monday

20 Friday

Manchester Beer & Cider Festival, Manchester

17 Tuesday

21 Saturday

Manchester Beer & Cider Festival, Manchester

18 Wednesday

22 Sunday

19 Thursday

Manchester Beer & Cider Festival, Manchester

Monday		2	9	16	23	30
Tuesday		3	10	17	24	31
Wednesday		4	11	18	25	
Thursday		5	12	19	26	
Friday		6	13	20	27	
Saturday		7	14	21	28	
Sunday	1	8	15	22	29	

Coopers Sparkling Ale (5.8%)

Coopers, Regency Park, South Australia

www.coopers.com.au

26th January – Australia Day

On 26 January 1788, Captain Arthur Phillip unfurled the British flag and formally laid claim to the colony of New South Wales, becoming its first governor. The day is now marked internationally as Australia Day, a vibrant celebration of all things Oz. Many of today's festivities will be lubricated only by bland Australian lagers that have become international commodities, but you really don't have to dig too deep to find beers from the country that are truly excellent.

It was in 1862 that Yorkshireman Thomas Cooper started brewing in Adelaide, South Australia, and the business has remained in the hands of his descendants ever since. The jewel in the company's crown remains a traditional pale ale of the kind Thomas himself brewed 150 years or so ago. It's called simply Sparkling Ale and it's been knocking around the international stage for several decades now, buoyed by its uniqueness during most of this period as a bottle-conditioned Australian beer. Sparkling Ale (5.8%) is noted for its hazy appearance as the fine sediment infiltrates the beer in the glass. It's fresh, it's fruity – with spicy, peppery pear notes emerging from the fermentation process and the combination of Saaz and Pride of Ringwood hops – and it's very refreshing. Other beers from the Coopers stable are available, too. So, if you're thinking of raising a cork-dangling hat to the Australian nation, remember that discerning Aussie drinkers wouldn't give a XXXX for a glass of the 'Amber Nectar'. They'd be seeking out a Coopers.

23 Monday

27 Friday

24 Tuesday

28 Saturday •
Chinese New Year

25 Wednesday
Burns Night

29 Sunday

26 Thursday

Monday		2	9	16	23	30
Tuesday		3	10	17	24	31
Wednesday		4	11	18	25	
Thursday		5	12	19	26	
Friday		6	13	20	27	
Saturday		7	14	21	28	
Sunday	1	8	15	22	29	

Bryncelyn Buddy Marvellous (4%)

Bryncelyn Brewery, Ystalyfera, Neath Port Talbot

Buddy Holly (left) and his band, the Crickets

3rd February – Buddy Holly dies, 1959

On the third day of February 1959, rock star Buddy Holly lost his life. Buddy and fellow rock stars Richie Valens and The Big Bopper chartered a small plane to take them from Clear Lake, Iowa, to Fargo, North Dakota, for a gig. They never made it. In bad weather, the plane crashed just a few minutes' after take-off. All three were killed. For many, this day has become known as 'the day the music died', but for Will Hopton, a young man in the South Wales valleys, it was the day a lifelong obsession began.

'I was a fan of Buddy Holly before then, but not really in a big way,' he recalls. 'But after the crash, I grew to appreciate the music more and more.' The Holly fascination has since grown and grown, to the point where Will has started a brewery and dedicated it to the late Texan singer.

Bryncelyn which translates from Welsh as 'Holly Hill', is a tiny brewery originally set up in the cellar of Will's pub, the Wern Fawr, in Ystalyfera, but now housed at a larger nearby site. It turns out a range of award-winning beers, all bearing a Buddy Holly connection, but the beer to savour today, perhaps with Buddy's Greatest Hits playing softly in the background, is Buddy Marvellous. This is a reddish, 4% Mild that was deservedly voted CAMRA's Champion Beer of Wales in 2002. Only gently bitter, the beer has a complex fruit and malt flavour, and enough body to be totally satisfying. Like Will's other beers, it's a classy and respectful tribute to one of music's greats.

30 Monday

31 Tuesday

1 Wednesday

2 Thursday

3 Friday

4 Saturday   ◑

5 Sunday

Monday		6	13	20	27
Tuesday		7	14	21	28
Wednesday	1	8	15	22	
Thursday	2	9	16	23	
Friday	3	10	17	24	
Saturday	4	11	18	25	
Sunday	5	12	19	26	

February 2017

Williams Bros Kelpie (4.4%)

Williams Bros Brewing Co., Alloa, Clackmannanshire

fraoch.com

Seaweed salad

6th February – Seaweed Day

It is indicative of the importance of the ocean to the economy and culture of Japan that the people celebrate an annual Seaweed Day. Originally, the day was instituted to commemorate an ancient law that decreed that seaweed – a culinary delicacy – was a fitting tribute to offer the Emperor. These days, it's a good excuse to munch sushi wrapped in nori.

We don't eat much seaweed in the West, although the Welsh have always had a way with laverbread. We don't sup much seaweed either, but judging from the taste of one Scottish beer that does include this maritime vegetable, we may be missing out.

The Williams Brothers, Bruce and Scott, have been digging up Scotland's brewing past since 1992. Several hundreds of years ago, coastal farmers in Scotland would grow barley used for brewing in fields fertilised by seaweed. Inevitably, this unusual practice had an influence on the flavour of the crop. The brothers have attempted to bring a little seaweed influence to their beer by bunging some bladderwrack into the mash tun while making a dark, rich brew – Kelpie – from organic barley. It turns out at only 4.4% ABV, but it's a full-value beer that doesn't really taste much of the ocean or its produce, except for a dry, savoury note with a little coffee breaking through in the finish.

A beer containing seaweed doesn't really sound too appealing, if we're honest, but take a leaf out of the Japanese book and give it a go. February 6 gives you an excuse.

6 Monday

7 Tuesday

8 Wednesday

9 Thursday

10 Friday

11 Saturday ○

12 Sunday

Monday		6	13	20	27
Tuesday		7	14	21	28
Wednesday	1	8	15	22	
Thursday	2	9	16	23	
Friday	3	10	17	24	
Saturday	4	11	18	25	
Sunday	5	12	19	26	

Harvey's Kiss (4.8%)

Harvey & Son, Lewes, East Sussex

www.harveys.org.uk

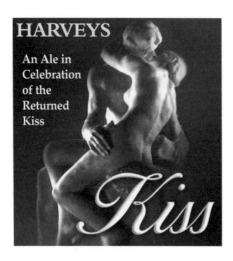

14th February – Valentine's Day

St Valentine's Day has to be one of the most widely celebrated of all saints' feast days. One of the many brewers producing a Valentine's Day beer is Harvey's in Sussex. But Harvey's beer is not a simple cash-in: it has its own tale to tell.

Auguste Rodin's famous sculpture The Kiss was commissioned by an American millionaire who owned a mansion at Lewes. He agreed to put it on show in the town in 1914. Rodin's work graphically illustrates two naked bodies entwined, so graphically in fact that local headmistress Miss Kate Fowler-Tutt publicly objected to its presence and succeeded in having the steamy statue removed from display. The work eventually ended up in the Tate Gallery in London, but in 1999 it was brought back to Lewes for a five-month visit to mark the arrival of the new millennium.

Harvey's Kiss was first brewed to celebrate the event, and has been brewed as a cask beer for St Valentine's Day ever since. The beer is golden in colour, with an aroma of pears and other cocktail fruit. The bittersweet taste has a mealy character from the oats and is slightly nutty, but perfumed floral notes and more pears dominate the palate, running on into the slightly warming, drying and gradually more bitter finish. It's the beer equivalent of a bouquet of St Valentine's Day flowers.

13 Monday

14 Tuesday

15 Wednesday

Chelmsford Winter Beer & Cider Festival,
Chelmsford, Essex

16 Thursday

Chelmsford Winter Beer & Cider Festival,
Chelmsford, Essex

17 Friday

Chelmsford Winter Beer & Cider Festival,
Chelmsford, Essex

18 Saturday ◑

Chelmsford Winter Beer & Cider Festival,
Chelmsford, Essex

19 Sunday

Monday		6	13	20	27
Tuesday		7	14	21	28
Wednesday	1	8	15	22	
Thursday	2	9	16	23	
Friday	3	10	17	24	
Saturday	4	11	18	25	
Sunday	5	12	19	26	

Flying Dog Gonzo Imperial Porter (9.2%)

Flying Dog Brewery, Frederick, Maryland

flyingdogbrewery.com

20th February – Hunter S Thompson dies, 2005

Every now and then a writer comes along who throws the rulebook out of the window and sets a fashion for others to follow. Hunter S Thompson was one. His journalistic style crashed through established barriers, culminating in what came to be termed the Gonzo style. This involves blurring the distinction between reality and fiction, and allowing personal input to influence the story.

His most famous book is *Fear and Loathing in Las Vegas*, a graphic account of a drug-crazed, hedonistic weekend in America's gambling capital in the early 1970s. He spent his last years in Aspen, Colorado. It was here that he took his own life in 2005, aged 67.

Thompson became a hero to many who enjoyed his acerbic approach to US culture and authority, and his name is remembered in a clutch of beers from the Flying Dog brewery, based in Frederick, Maryland. This is more than just a collection of tribute brews, however. Thompson was an old friend and beer buddy of brewery co-founder George Stranahan. Their association eventually created the first 'Gonzo beer', with labels drawn by Thompson's long-term illustrator Ralph Steadman and graced with the Thompson quote that 'good people drink good beer'. Gonzo Imperial Porter is probably the easiest to track down, a mighty 9% brew. Like Thompson it is bold and outspoken, belting out 80 units of bitterness. According to Flying Dog, the beer is 'dry hopped with a shit load of Cascade hops' and should be drunk 'wherever fear and loathing strike'.

Hunter S Thompson

20 Monday

21 Tuesday

22 Wednesday

National Winter Ales Festival, Norwich, Norfolk

23 Thursday

National Winter Ales Festival, Norwich, Norfolk

24 Friday

National Winter Ales Festival, Norwich, Norfolk

25 Saturday

National Winter Ales Festival, Norwich, Norfolk

26 Sunday ●

Monday		6	13	20	27
Tuesday		7	14	21	28
Wednesday	1	8	15	22	
Thursday	2	9	16	23	
Friday	3	10	17	24	
Saturday	4	11	18	25	
Sunday	5	12	19	26	

Früh Kölsch (4.8%)

Cölner Hofbräu Früh, Cologne

frueh.de

The Rose Monday parade at Cologne Carnival

27th February – Cologne Carnival

Anyone who believes that there are only four seasons in the year should pay a visit to Cologne. The locals there celebrate five. The 'Fifth Season' is a period of merriment that begins on 11 November. It is, in fact, a long, drawn-out prelude to Easter, and it comes to a head with the world-famous Cologne Carnival.

After the November launch, things quieten down somewhat until the approach of Lent, when the city erupts in what are known as the 'Crazy Days'. These kick off on a Thursday, with fancy dress and masked balls. Partying continues over the weekend, with pubs and bars open way beyond their regular hours, and then reaches its zenith on Rose Monday (the day before Shrove Tuesday). This is when the big official procession takes to the streets, headed by the leading Carnival figures of the Prince, the Peasant and the Maiden.

Beer, as in most areas of German life, plays an important role in the Cologne Carnival. The city has its own particular beer style, called Kölsch, after the local name for the city, Köln. If you're looking to re-create a touch of carnival atmosphere at home, then seek out one of the best exported versions: Früh Kölsch. The beer has a very pale golden colour, which belies its flavour-packed taste. Typically lively on the palate, the beer is pleasantly bitter with a smooth malt backdrop and lemon and spicy-herbal notes from the hops. The finish is moreishly hoppy. Floral, fruity and fun – it's all a Kölsch is meant to be.

27 Monday

3 Friday

28 Tuesday
Shrove Tuesday

4 Saturday

1 Wednesday
St David's Day, Ash Wednesday

5 Sunday ◑

2 Thursday

Monday	27	6	13	20	27
Tuesday	28	7	14	21	28
Wednesday	1	8	15	22	
Thursday	2	9	16	23	
Friday	3	10	17	24	
Saturday	4	11	18	25	
Sunday	5	12	19	26	

March 2017

Orval (6.2%)

Brasserie d'Orval, Villers-devant-Orval

orval.be

The abbey at Villers-devant-Orval

9th March – Orval joins the Cistercian order, 1132

There is no beer in the world like Orval. It's such a delicate blend of malt, hop and assertive, acidic dryness that anyone attempting to re-create the magic is sure to slip up somewhere along the way.

The beer is brewed by the brothers at Orval abbey, a religious settlement in Belgium's Ardennes forest. The site dates back to the 11th century, when monks from Italy made a base here. In 1076, a visiting countess, Mathilda of Tuscany, lost her wedding ring in a gushing spring in the grounds. She prayed to the Virgin Mary for its safe return, only to find a trout rising to the surface carrying the ring in its mouth. Her jubilation led her to declare the site 'a golden valley' ('orval'). For some unknown reason, the original monks fled not long after, leaving control of the abbey to local church workers. They fell into financial distress and applied to the Cistercian body of friars for assistance. They were accepted into the order and, on 9 March 1132, seven monks arrived to refashion the church.

Orval's brewery was re-established in 1931. It brews only one beer for commercial sale. Water comes from Mathilda's original spring, pale and caramel malts are used in the mash, and Hallertau and Styrian Golding hops provide the seasoning. Crucially, a small dosage of *brettanomyces* yeast is also introduced. This endows Orval with its remarkable dry, acidic character, and a saintly status among beer lovers.

6 Monday

10 Friday

7 Tuesday

11 Saturday

8 Wednesday

12 Sunday   ○
Purim

9 Thursday

Monday		6	13	20	27
Tuesday		7	14	21	28
Wednesday	1	8	15	22	29
Thursday	2	9	16	23	30
Friday	3	10	17	24	31
Saturday	4	11	18	25	
Sunday	5	12	19	26	

Paulaner Salvator (7.9%)

Paulaner, Munich

paulaner.de

19th March – Starkbierzeit in Munich

If you're tempted to visit the Oktoberfest but are daunted by the crowds, then maybe March in Munich is a better option. Beginning on St Joseph's Day, the city marks the end of winter with a strong beer season, known as the Starkbierzeit. The origins of the Starkbierzeit lie with the monks who founded what is today Paulaner Brewery. They brewed beer largely for their own consumption, including a strong beer specifically fashioned for sustenance during Lent, when solid food was prohibited. The beer was known by a number of religious names but eventually settled down under the title of Salvator, or saviour. When this strong lager went on sale to the public, it proved extremely popular, and other breweries clamoured to make their own versions. The style created by Salvator has become known as doppelbock.

Salvator pours a welcoming russet colour and brings a cleanness to the palate that only a long lagering period can achieve. It is steeped in sweet, raisin-fruity malt and hop flavours with a light toffee undercurrent. As the monks who brewed it first knew only too well, it is a meal in a glass, and yet somewhat belies its 7.9% alcohol.

On 19 March each year, celebrities and politicians gather for the ceremonial opening of Starkbierzeit in Paulaner's bier keller on top of Munich's highest hill. A cask of Salvator is tapped amid great festivity, and the locals, foaming jugs in hand, toast the fact that the hard Bavarian winter is hopefully behind them. Don't worry if you can't make it to Munich though, a glass of Salvator will take the chill off a March day anywhere in the world.

13 Monday

17 Friday

Leeds Beer, Cider & Perry Festival, Leeds, West Yorkshire
St Patrick's Day
Public holiday Northern Ireland

14 Tuesday

18 Saturday

Leeds Beer, Cider & Perry Festival, Leeds, West Yorkshire

15 Wednesday

19 Sunday

16 Thursday

Leeds Beer, Cider & Perry Festival, Leeds, West Yorkshire

Monday		6	13	20	27
Tuesday		7	14	21	28
Wednesday	1	8	15	22	29
Thursday	2	9	16	23	30
Friday	3	10	17	24	31
Saturday	4	11	18	25	
Sunday	5	12	19	26	

March 2017

Durham St Cuthbert (6.5%)

The Durham Brewery, Bowburn, Co. Durham

durham-brewery.co.uk

20th March – St Cuthbert's Day

Today is the feast day of the patron saint of Northumbria. St Cuthbert was born around the year 634, in what these days would be termed the Scottish Borders. He is said to have given his life to God after seeing St Aidan, Bishop of Lindisfarne, being transported to heaven in a blaze of light. Thereafter, Cuthbert travelled the region and further afield, preaching and helping the disadvantaged. He was himself appointed Bishop of Lindisfarne but much preferred a hermit's existence, and many of his years were spent in solitude on the Farne Islands, which is where he died on 20 March 687. After his death, the monks that he had inspired fled with his body and finally settled in what is now the city of Durham.

St Cuthbert's remains still lie in the awesome, dimly lit cathedral in Durham, and his name is celebrated in a top-quality beer from a local brewery. Durham Brewery was founded in 1994 by former music teachers Steve and Christine Gibbs. Many of their beers are named after Durham and its religious connections. St Cuthbert is an IPA in style, light amber in colour and with a full aroma of orange and toffeeish malt, thanks to a recipe that includes crystal and wheat malts, and no fewer than five different strains of hop. Challenger, Target, Columbus, Golding and Saaz combine with the malt to produce a bittersweet, citrus taste, with pear drop notes pointing to the considerable strength (6.5%), before a soft, bitter finish.

St Cuthbert's Cross, Alnmouth

20 Monday ◐

21 Tuesday

22 Wednesday

23 Thursday

Bristol Beer Festival, Bristol

24 Friday

Bristol Beer Festival, Bristol

25 Saturday

Bristol Beer Festival, Bristol

26 Sunday

Daylight Saving Time starts, Mothering Sunday

Monday		6	13	20	27
Tuesday		7	14	21	28
Wednesday	1	8	15	22	29
Thursday	2	9	16	23	30
Friday	3	10	17	24	31
Saturday	4	11	18	25	
Sunday	5	12	19	26	

Young's Special (4.5%)

Charles Wells, Bedford

charleswells.co.uk

The Queen Mother on a famous visit to the Queens Head

30th March – Queen Mother dies, 2002

When Royalty pays a ceremonial visit to a pub, you don't expect it to nip behind the bar and start pulling a pint. But that's what happened when Queen Elizabeth, the Queen Mother, attended a function at the Queens Head pub in Stepney in 1987. It was a memorable moment in the history of Young's, which owned the pub, and they recorded it in a famous photograph that found its way onto the walls of other pubs in the brewery's estate.

Elizabeth was wife of Prince Albert, who became King George VI in 1936 on the abdication of his brother, King Edward VIII. On his own death in 1952, he was succeeded by their daughter, Elizabeth, with his wife taking on the title and position of Queen Mother. It was a role Elizabeth (senior) played to perfection, judging from the fondness with which she was regarded by the British people.

In light of her relationship with the people of Britain, it is appropriate that the beer she has become associated with is called Special. Although now brewed by Charles Wells, it has long been one of the jewels in the Young's crown, with a fine balance between malt and hops, and a dry, bitter aftertaste. The malts are Maris Otter pale and crystal, and the hops are Fuggle and Golding. In this respect it's about as traditional a British beer as you can find, and a good choice with which to remember a popular lady.

27 Monday

31 Friday

28 Tuesday   •

1 Saturday

29 Wednesday

2 Sunday

30 Thursday

Monday		6	13	20	27
Tuesday		7	14	21	28
Wednesday	1	8	15	22	29
Thursday	2	9	16	23	30
Friday	3	10	17	24	31
Saturday	4	11	18	25	1
Sunday	5	12	19	26	2

April 2017

Belvoir Melton Red (4.3%)

Belvoir Brewery, Old Dalby, Leicestershire

belvoirbrewery.co.uk

6th April – Painting the town red, 1837

On 6 April 1837, the Marquis of Waterford enjoyed a drunken day out at Croxton Park racecourse in Leicestershire. Not one to know when he'd taken a drop too much, the Marquis then led his coterie of sycophants back to the town of Melton Mowbray where he was staying for the night. Chaos ensued as the drunken toffs ran amok in the streets, fighting, singing and generally making a nuisance of themselves. The highlight of their evening was the acquisition of some red paint, which they proceeded to daub over the buildings of the town. When the night was over, a good time had been had by all – locals apart – and the Marquis and his louts had become the first people to 'paint the town red'.

So is this really the origin of that well-worn phrase? Melton locals cling to the story, and when buildings were refurbished in the town in the 1980s, ancient red paint was discovered beneath the surface plaster.

Using the tale to good effect is Belvoir Brewery, which was founded in 1995 by former Shipstone's and Theakston's brewer Colin Brown. The brewery is located in the village of Old Dalby, between Melton Mowbray and Loughborough, in the beautiful Vale of Belvoir (pronounced 'beaver'). Melton Red was introduced in 2002. The beer is amber in colour – the result of combining pale and crystal malts, plus a little torrefied wheat – and has a dry, malty, bitter flavour with a toffee note, a little orchard fruit and some herbal hop character, courtesy of a complex mix of five hops – Target, Bramling Cross, Progress, Golding and Styrian Golding. It's not available in cask form, only in bottle.

3 Monday ◑

7 Friday

CAMRA Members' Weekend, Bournemouth, Dorset

4 Tuesday

8 Saturday

CAMRA Members' Weekend, Bournemouth, Dorset

5 Wednesday

9 Sunday

CAMRA Members' Weekend, Bournemouth, Dorset
Palm Sunday

6 Thursday

Monday		3	10	17	24
Tuesday		4	11	18	25
Wednesday		5	12	19	26
Thursday		6	13	20	27
Friday		7	14	21	28
Saturday	1	8	15	22	29
Sunday	2	9	16	23	30

Traquair Jacobite Ale (8%)

Traquair House Brewery, Innerleithen, Peeblesshire

traquair.co.uk

16th April – Battle of Culloden, 1746

Traquair's Jacobite Ale is a celebration of the Jacobite cause: the rebellion of the followers of the Stuarts in the 17th and 18th century, when they attempted to restore a member of the family to the British throne. Leader of the most famous uprising was Charles Edward Stuart, otherwise known as Bonnie Prince Charlie, grandson of the deposed King James II of England.

Bonnie Prince Charlie decided to retake the throne by force. From exile in Italy, he assembled an army and invaded England. His support came largely from the Highlands, where the clan system saw him guaranteed plenty of supporters. After a foray into England, the forces were made to turn back and, eventually, the adventure came to an end on this day in 1746, when the Jacobite Rebellion was snuffed out in a brief but bloody battle at Culloden, near Inverness. After just over an hour's fighting, around 1,200 men lay dead.

Bonnie Prince Charlie unceremoniously fled the scene, never to return, although the romance of the Stuarts lingers still in places such as Traquair House. The stately home on the Scottish Borders had played host to Charles when he arrived in 1745, and its Bear Gates were locked shut after he left, never to open again until a Stuart once more sits on the throne. The Jacobite Ale brewed at its on-site brewery is sweet and malty in the Scottish tradition, but not heavy, in spite of its 8% strength, with a soft spiciness. It is brewed from an 18th-century recipe, laced with coriander, and makes a far better case for the Stuarts and their cause than any amount of pointless bloodshed.

10 Monday

14 Friday
Good Friday
Public holiday UK

11 Tuesday   ○
First day of Passover

15 Saturday

12 Wednesday

16 Sunday

13 Thursday

Monday		3	10	17	24
Tuesday		4	11	18	25
Wednesday		5	12	19	26
Thursday		6	13	20	27
Friday		7	14	21	28
Saturday	1	8	15	22	29
Sunday	2	9	16	23	30

Rodenbach Grand Cru (6%)

Brouwerij Rodenbach, Roeselare

rodenbach.be

22nd April – Zythos Beer Festival, Belgium

Belgium is a country that offers hundreds of fascinating breweries. Between them they create thousands of beers, and only a visit to the country gives a true flavour of what it's all about. But there are only so many beers you can take in one session – especially at Belgian strength.

Fortunately there is a place where they all come together. The largest beer festival in Belgium is hosted by Zythos, the Belgian equivalent of CAMRA, and is staged in the town of Leuven, 20km (12 miles) east of Brussels. The great benefit of the event is that beers are sold in small samples, so you can stroll around the room tasting Belgium in a day.

When you arrive at the venue, you'll be confronted by a mind-boggling selection of more than 300 Belgian beers, supplied by around 80 breweries. The added bonus is that beers are often served by the brewers themselves, so you can chat to the makers about their products.

We can't all make it to Leuven, so here's a giant on the Belgian stage that will provide plenty of consolation comfort. The Rodenbach brewery in Roeselare, was founded in the 1820s. Its speciality has always been oak-aged sour red beers, which were once described by beer writer Michael Jackson as 'the world's most refreshing'. Whenever I go to Belgium, Rodenbach is often the first beer I call for, its tart fruit flavours and acetic bite sharpening the palate and setting me up for some of the heavier beers to come. Its idiosyncrasy is typical of the Belgian brewing industry as a whole.

17 Monday

Easter Monday
Public holiday England, Wales & Northern Ireland

18 Tuesday

Last day of Passover

19 Wednesday ☽

20 Thursday

21 Friday

22 Saturday

Zythos Bierfestival, Leuven, Belgium

23 Sunday

St George's Day
Zythos Bierfestival, Leuven, Belgium

Monday		3	10	17	24
Tuesday		4	11	18	25
Wednesday		5	12	19	26
Thursday		6	13	20	27
Friday		7	14	21	28
Saturday	1	8	15	22	29
Sunday	2	9	16	23	30

Little Creatures Pale Ale (5.2%)

Little Creatures Brewing, Fremantle

littlecreatures.com.au

ANZAC Day parade in Melbourne

25th April – ANZAC Day

The 25th day of April is ANZAC Day, when the citizens of Australia and New Zealand pay tribute to their compatriots who have died in war. The roots of the day can be found in World War I, when Australian and New Zealand forces worked together to play their part in defeating Germany. On 25 April 1915, the ANZACs (Australia and New Zealand Army Corps) spearheaded a mission to capture Constantinople (now Istanbul) and open up access to the Black Sea. Their bridgehead was a beach at Gallipoli, and the aim was a quick, pre-emptive strike that would catch the Turks, allies of the Germans, unawares. Things didn't go to plan, however. Turkish resistance was fierce, and the campaign waged for eight months before the ANZACs withdrew, thousands of men having lost their lives in the conflict.

If a glass is to be raised in respect and memory of the men who died in this and other campaigns, then it needs to be filled with something special. That something special could be Little Creatures Pale Ale.

Little Creatures comes from a brewery and pub founded in 2000 in Fremantle, Western Australia. What lifts the beer out of the ordinary is the use of American whole-leaf hops. They don't go into the copper, instead, they sit in the wort in a giant 'tea bag' so the big floral, fruity flavours from the Cascade and Chinook hops soak into the beer just before fermentation begins. There's a good, clean freshness to the whole drink. Tangy, peppery hops feature prominently in the taste, along with spritzy grapefruit notes and other citrus fruit.

24 Monday

28 Friday
Hull Real Ale & Cider Festival, Hull, East Yorkshire;
Newcastle Beer & Cider Festival, Newcastle, Tyne & Wear

25 Tuesday

29 Saturday
Hull Real Ale & Cider Festival, Hull, East Yorkshire;
Newcastle Beer & Cider Festival, Newcastle, Tyne & Wear

26 Wednesday ●
Newcastle Beer & Cider Festival, Newcastle, Tyne & Wear

30 Sunday

27 Thursday
Hull Real Ale & Cider Festival, Hull, East Yorkshire;
Newcastle Beer & Cider Festival, Newcastle, Tyne & Wear

Monday		3	10	17	24
Tuesday		4	11	18	25
Wednesday		5	12	19	26
Thursday		6	13	20	27
Friday		7	14	21	28
Saturday	1	8	15	22	29
Sunday	2	9	16	23	30

Brains SA Gold (4.3%)

S A Brain & Co. Ltd, Cardiff

sabrain.com

Brains founder
Samuel Arthur Brain

4th May – Samuel Arthur Brain born, 1850

It's impossible to visit the capital of Wales without noticing that the city is home to a major brewery. Nearly every pub displays its unusual name, and, where one doesn't, billboards and buses fill in the gap.

Brains Brewery has its origins in this day in 1850, with the birth of co-founder Samuel Arthur Brain. Samuel Arthur arrived in Cardiff in the early 1860s and trained as a brewer at the local Phoenix Brewery. He was keen, however, to plough his own furrow. In 1882, Samuel drew on the financial assistance of his uncle, Joseph Benjamin Brain, to acquire Cardiff's Old Brewery. With SA Brain at the helm, the business flourished, and five years later a new brewhouse was constructed on the same site. Brain himself became a notable figure in local society, as a city councillor and later Mayor of Cardiff. He died in 1903, at the age of only 52, but the Brain family is still at the helm of the brewery.

The company now runs more than 250 pubs and produces a wide range of beers. The perennial favourite has always been the beer named simply SA, in honour of the founder. The SA brand was extended in 2006, with the creation of a new blonde ale called SA Gold. This is a beer with a more modern image, cashing in on the trend for straw-coloured beers. It's SA Gold that is today's selection, as it conveniently links the long history of the company with the dynamism and foresight shown by the present management. They've turned the local drink of Cardiff into the national beer of Wales and that's no mean achievement.

1 Monday
Beltane, *Public holiday UK*

2 Tuesday

3 Wednesday ◑

4 Thursday

5 Friday

6 Saturday

7 Sunday

Monday	1	8	15	22	29
Tuesday	2	9	16	23	30
Wednesday	3	10	17	24	31
Thursday	4	11	18	25	
Friday	5	12	19	26	
Saturday	6	13	20	27	
Sunday	7	14	21	28	

Batemans Victory Ale (6%)

Batemans Brewery, Wainfleet, Lincolnshire

bateman.co.uk

Londoners celebrate VE Day in 1945

8th May – VE Day

This day, 8 May 1945, will forever just be known as VE Day. After nearly six years of warfare, Nazi Germany was finally defeated and Victory in Europe was declared. It was understandably a day for enormous celebration, jubilation as well as quiet respect for those that fell during the conflict. Savouring a glass of beer named Victory is clearly an appropriate way to note the occasion, although the beer selected here was actually brewed for quite a different success. The label currently depicts Admiral Nelson and his flagship, also of course called *Victory*, but the beer was created for events rather closer to home.

In the mid-1980s, family-owned Batemans entered a period of great instability. Shares of the company were split between Chairman George Bateman and his brother and sister, John and Helen. When John and Helen announced that they wanted to sell the brewery and cash in their shares, George was appalled.

After many fraught months, George was able to raise the funds to buy out his siblings. So Batemans remained in brewing, with George at the helm, and to celebrate their success in a battle for independence, the Batemans created Victory Ale in October 1987.

At 6% ABV, Victory is an ale to respect. Brewed from Maris Otter pale malt, some crystal malt and Golding and Liberty hops, it's full-bodied and malty, with plenty of hop character and the Batemans trademark banana-like yeastiness. It's rarely available in cask form these days, but you can always find it in bottle.

8 Monday

12 Friday

9 Tuesday

13 Saturday

10 Wednesday   ○

14 Sunday

11 Thursday

Monday	1	8	15	22	29
Tuesday	2	9	16	23	30
Wednesday	3	10	17	24	31
Thursday	4	11	18	25	
Friday	5	12	19	26	
Saturday	6	13	20	27	
Sunday	7	14	21	28	

Dartmoor Jail Ale (4.8%)

Dartmoor Brewery Ltd, Princetown, Devon

dartmoorbrewery.co.uk

English social reformer Elizabeth Fry

21st May – Elizabeth Fry born, 1780

The debate on prison reform has been raging for over 200 years, thanks largely to the intervention of Elizabeth Fry, who was born today in 1780.

Visiting Newgate Prison in 1813, Fry was appalled at the conditions in which hundreds of women and children were living, some of whom had never even been tried for any crime. Crammed into small cells, the inmates lived a life of extreme misery. Fry set up schools for the imprisoned children and encouraged the women to acquire new skills. She published a report into the prison situation, spoke to a House of Commons committee and even received audiences with Queen Victoria. Her actions made life more bearable for thousands of inmates.

There is no beer that directly celebrates Fry's life or her legacy, but there is a very fine beer that shares a connection with one of Britain's most famous prisons. Built in 1809, Dartmoor Prison at Princetown, Devon, was first used to house French and American prisoners of war. It became a criminal jail in 1850 and suffered a reputation for being a particularly austere place in which to serve time. As Fry would have hoped, much has been done in recent years to change this image.

Just along the road from the prison is Dartmoor Brewery, whose star performer over the years has been Jail Ale. It pours an enticing dark golden colour and offers clean, bittersweet, fruity, floral flavours, thanks to the generous seasoning of Challenger and Progress hops.

I doubt if Dartmoor ever had Elizabeth Fry in mind when it devised the beer, but the names of those hops are certainly appropriate when it comes to remembering her life and her influence.

15 Monday

19 Friday ◑

16 Tuesday

20 Saturday

17 Wednesday

21 Sunday

18 Thursday

Monday	1	8	15	22	29
Tuesday	2	9	16	23	30
Wednesday	3	10	17	24	31
Thursday	4	11	18	25	
Friday	5	12	19	26	
Saturday	6	13	20	27	
Sunday	7	14	21	28	

Van Steenberge Piraat (10.5%)

Brewery Van Steenberge, Ertvelde

vansteenberge.com

Captain William Kidd hanging in chains

23rd May – Captain Kidd dies, 1701

One of the best-known beers from the family-run Van Steenberge brewery in Ertvelde, Belgium, is called Piraat, or pirate. It's an appropriate choice, as this was the day that one of the most notorious pirates finally met his maker.

William Kidd was born in Scotland, around 1645, but moved to America while still a young boy. Much of his seafaring career appears to have been respectable: he was granted a licence as a privateer, intercepting ships belonging to the enemies of Britain, with the proceeds of the haul shared with the Crown.

Unfortunately Kidd's crew mutinied when they realised that he planned to ignore vessels belonging to friendly countries, even though they had bounty to spare. To keep his rebellious men on side, it seems, Kidd fell into the ways of a common pirate. He was captured, tried, and sent to the gallows on this day in 1701, vainly protesting his innocence and promising, if released, to retrieve a secret haul of treasure he had hidden and give it to the government. The treasure has never been found.

Van Steenberge's Piraat follows in the long tradition of strong beers that were brewed to be taken out to sea. It comes in two forms, a stronger version at 10.5% and the more common 9%. I would imagine that pirates would opt for the higher-strength version, which certainly doesn't pull any punches. The perfumed aroma is filled with cutlass-sharp, zesty orange notes, which pop up again in the crisp taste, along with light herbal notes. The finish is drying, bittersweet, perfumed, hoppy and as warming as a daily ration of grog.

22 Monday
Cambridge Beer Festival, Cambridge

23 Tuesday
Cambridge Beer Festival, Cambridge

24 Wednesday
Cambridge Beer Festival, Cambridge

25 Thursday
Cambridge Beer Festival, Cambridge

26 Friday
Cambridge Beer Festival, Cambridge

27 Saturday
Cambridge Beer Festival, Cambridge
Ramadan begins

28 Sunday

Monday	1	8	15	22	29
Tuesday	2	9	16	23	30
Wednesday	3	10	17	24	31
Thursday	4	11	18	25	
Friday	5	12	19	26	
Saturday	6	13	20	27	
Sunday	7	14	21	28	

Warwickshire Lady Godiva (4.2%)

The Warwickshire Beer Co., Cubbington, Warwickshire

www.warwickshirebeer.co.uk

31st May – Lady Godiva procession inaugurated, 1678

Today we suggest that you raise a glass to an event that almost certainly never took place. But it's a good tale anyway. Back in the 11th century, beautiful Godiva was the wife of Leofric, Earl of Mercia. Being rather closer to the people than her husband, Godiva was concerned at the harsh taxes ordinary citizens were expected to pay, and raised the issue with her other half. His response, allegedly, was that he would lower taxes if she rode through the streets of Coventry naked. Surprisingly, she agreed and, wearing nothing but her birthday suit, Godiva climbed aboard her horse and proceeded through the city.

It's highly unlikely that any of the above happened. There is more evidence, however, that on 31 May 1678, the people of Coventry latched onto the legend by instigating a lively Godiva procession. The event became very popular, especially in the 19th century, when Godiva's route took in many of the city's pubs, leading to accusations that the lovely lady was often drunk on duty. The procession still takes place today and has led to a full-blown Godiva festival, a major occasion for free music of all kinds and other family entertainment, now staged in July.

One of the local breweries also plays its part in keeping the myth alive. Warwickshire Beer Company's Lady Godiva is a 4.2% dark golden ale, available in both cask and bottled versions. It is brewed from Maris Otter pale malt with crystal malt and some torrefied wheat. First Gold and Bobek hops provide the seasoning.

29 Monday

Public holiday UK

30 Tuesday

31 Wednesday

1 Thursday   ◑

Stockport Beer and Cider Festival,
Stockport, Greater Manchester

2 Friday

Stockport Beer and Cider Festival,
Stockport, Greater Manchester

3 Saturday

Stockport Beer and Cider Festival,
Stockport, Greater Manchester

4 Sunday

Monday	29	5	12	19	26
Tuesday	30	6	13	20	27
Wednesday	31	7	14	21	28
Thursday	1	8	15	22	29
Friday	2	9	16	23	30
Saturday	3	10	17	24	
Sunday	4	11	18	25	

Pitfield Eco Warrior (4.5%)

Pitfield Brewery, Moreton, Essex

dominionbrewerycompany.com

Tree planting in Damascus

5th June – World Environment Day

With the world only recently waking up to the threat of global warming and other environmental concerns, it's surprising to learn that the first World Environment Day was staged as long ago as 1972. The event is organized by the United Nations and was inaugurated during a related conference in Stockholm. A different city hosts the main event every year. Concerts, rallies, cycle rides, school festivities, clean-up campaigns, recycling initiatives and tree plantings are used to 'give a human face to environmental issues'. Therefore 5 June is the day to make peace with the planet.

The world of beer has made great strides towards sustainability in the last decade. Breweries are now being designed to be energy-efficient, with significantly lower gas, electricity and water usage. Some breweries have gone an extra mile and started producing organic beers. There are now several wholly organic breweries in the UK, such as Butts in Berkshire and Little Valley in West Yorkshire.

Pitfield Brewery has been at the forefront of organic beer development. The brewery started off in London but has now decamped to rural Essex where its organic credentials sit rather more comfortably than in the exhaust-choked capital. Not all of Pitfield's beers are organic, but the majority are, including the pioneering Eco Warrior. First brewed in 1998, this premium golden ale has always been a step ahead of the organic game. Pale malt and Hallertau hops are the main ingredients, conjuring between them a delicate sweetness overlaid by soft orangey-peachy fruit that becomes gradually more bitter.

5 Monday

9 Friday ○

6 Tuesday

10 Saturday

7 Wednesday

11 Sunday

8 Thursday

Monday		5	12	19	26
Tuesday		6	13	20	27
Wednesday		7	14	21	28
Thursday	1	8	15	22	29
Friday	2	9	16	23	30
Saturday	3	10	17	24	
Sunday	4	11	18	25	

Eggenberg Nessie (5%)

Brauerei Schloss Eggenberg, Vorchdorf

www.schloss-eggenberg.at

Nessie souvenir at Loch Ness

17th June – Loch Ness Monster sighted three times, 1993

Twenty three miles long, Loch Ness is a narrow but very deep, freshwater lake running south from Inverness in the Scottish Highlands. It's been the source of some unusual activity for centuries, with the 750ft depth of murky water declared to be home to at least one member of a long-forgotten species of water creature.

Eyewitnesses to the creature's behaviour describe it in various ways, but, generally, the impression created is one of a 30–40ft serpent-like creature with at least one hump, a small head and a maned neck. Scientific expeditions have probed the waters of Loch Ness, with mixed results, but the sightings have continued. Indeed, on 17 June 1993, three separate sightings of 'Nessie' were reported, by four different people. One of the witnesses, Edna MacInnes, even claimed she ran along the shore to keep up with the swimming beast, always in fear that she might be caught by the heavy wash it was generating.

The creature's global fame is underscored by the fact that its name has also been borrowed by a brewery in Austria for one of its beers. Nessie has been brewed since the early 1980s by the family-run Eggenberg Brewery, which sits in its own stunning lakeland between Salzburg and Vienna. The name seems appropriate for an unusual brew created, in part, out of Highland malt that is normally reserved for whisky making. The result is a dark golden, smoky-peaty ale of 5% ABV. It's fairly sweet and has a toffee note over a background of whisky and lemon. It would be a fine alternative to a warming dram during a night-time vigil at the side of Scotland's most famous watercourse.

12 Monday

16 Friday

13 Tuesday

17 Saturday ◑

14 Wednesday

18 Sunday
Father's Day

15 Thursday

Monday		5	12	19	26
Tuesday		6	13	20	27
Wednesday		7	14	21	28
Thursday	1	8	15	22	29
Friday	2	9	16	23	30
Saturday	3	10	17	24	
Sunday	4	11	18	25	

Stonehenge Heel Stone (4.3%)

Stonehenge Ales, Netheravon, Wiltshire

stonehengeales.co.uk

Midsummer sun rising over the Heel Stone

21st June – Summer solstice

In the northern hemisphere, 21 June marks the summer solstice, the day when the sun is at its highest point in the sky. In the UK, most attention during the summer solstice focuses on Stonehenge. This prehistoric collection of stones has confused analysts for centuries. There are still disputes over the specific purpose of the construction, with one of the most fascinating theories relating to its use as an astronomical clock. Every summer solstice, the sun, as it rises, climbs directly above the so-called Heel Stone, a single block that sits outside the main circle of stones. Thousands of people now descend on Stonehenge for the summer solstice to witness this rare dawn spectacle.

There are numerous theories as to the origin of the name Heel Stone. At their most literal, they refer to an occasion when the Devil threw the stone at a friar, hitting him on the heel. The Heel Stone is also celebrated in the name of a cask beer from Stonehenge brewery. Their Heel Stone is a light-bodied, copper-coloured best bitter. It has a malty, spicy nose that is followed in the mouth by a sweet spiciness from the hops over a clean, malty foundation. The finish is dry, malty, hoppy and decidedly moreish. Pale malt, crystal malt and wheat malt form the grist, while the hops are First Gold, Willamette and Bramling Cross, which may introduce a hint of blackcurrant to the aroma and taste. If you do join the early morning throngs hoping to catch a glimpse of the sun as it rises above the Heel Stone, there can be no more pertinent beer to seek out for a lunchtime pint afterwards.

19 Monday

23 Friday

20 Tuesday

24 Saturday •

21 Wednesday
Summer solstice

25 Sunday

22 Thursday

Monday		5	12	19	26
Tuesday		6	13	20	27
Wednesday		7	14	21	28
Thursday	1	8	15	22	29
Friday	2	9	16	23	30
Saturday	3	10	17	24	
Sunday	4	11	18	25	

Unibroue Blanche de Chambly (5%)

Unibroue Inc., Chambly, Quebec

unibroue.com

Canada Day celebrations in Calgary

1st July – Canada Day

It may be seen by some as the US's quieter neighbour, but Canada is no second-class citizen, as the people of the country will loudly tell you, especially on this day, its national day.

Canada's history dates back to Asian tribes that crossed the frozen Bering Strait. European influence had to wait until the arrival of the French in the 15th century, followed by the British. While, at first, both countries existed amicably, the Seven Years' War (1756–1763) between them spilled over into their North American territories and soured relationships. In 1867, the Governor General gave the land a new start, when all territories were joined together under a federal government. On 1 July, the British dominion of Canada was established – the source of the celebrations now known as Canada Day.

The French-speaking contingent of Canadians is still based in the province of Quebec. Here Unibroue, one of the country's best-known breweries also has its home. Any one of their beers is a worthy drink to savour for a taste of Canada today, but I've opted for Blanche de Chambly.

Blanche is a cloudy wheat beer. It contains both malted and raw wheat, alongside barley malt, and, true to style, is only lightly hopped, leaving the character to emerge from the selection of secret spices that flavour the brew. The beer pours a pale golden colour. The aroma is fresh and appealing, slightly bready and laced with lemon-citrus notes. The same citrus accent is obvious in the taste, which is bittersweet and lemon-sharp with a suggestion of malty toffee behind. More of the same flavours run into the dry, bready finish.

26 Monday

Eid-al-Fitr

30 Friday

27 Tuesday

1 Saturday ◑

28 Wednesday

2 Sunday

29 Thursday

Monday		5	12	19	26
Tuesday		6	13	20	27
Wednesday		7	14	21	28
Thursday	1	8	15	22	29
Friday	2	9	16	23	30
Saturday	3	10	17	24	1
Sunday	4	11	18	25	2

Okell's MacLir (4.4%)

Okell's Ltd, Douglas

www.okells.co.uk

5th July – National Day, Isle of Man

Because of its geography, language, currency and general way of life, it's commonly assumed that the Isle of Man is a part of the United Kingdom. It's not. While the British monarch is officially the head of state, this island, halfway between Lancashire and Northern Ireland, is in fact an independent kingdom, something that is celebrated every 5 July.

On this day, the Tynwald, or Manx parliament, rises from its normal debating house in the capital, Douglas, and holds a ceremonial open-air session on Tynwald Hill, a terraced, circular mound in the village of St John's. Bills that have passed through the legislature are promulgated on this occasion, petitions are received, and the opportunity is taken to swear in important officials. It is a day to celebrate being a Manxman – perhaps with a glass of local beer.

The main brewery on the island is Okell's, which was founded by Dr William Okell in 1850. Brewing now takes place in a state-of-the-art brewhouse just outside Douglas, and the range of ales includes a wheat beer called MacLir, which – as its name unintentionally suggests – pours bright rather than cloudy. It's actually named after Manannán Mac Lir, a Norse god of the sea, who once was said to be a protector of the island. The beer contains 50% barley malt and 50% wheat malt. Wheat was something previously prohibited under the terms of the famous Manx Pure Beer Act, which meant that Okell's needed to apply to the Tynwald for permission for its use. The resultant beer is broadly in the style of a Belgian witbier, golden in colour and laced with abundant peppery, bitter, zesty lime-like flavours that make it so refreshing, especially on a warm July day.

The Tynwald holding an open-air session

3 Monday

4 Tuesday
Chelmsford Summer Beer & Cider Festival,
Chelmsford, Essex

5 Wednesday
Chelmsford Summer Beer & Cider Festival,
Chelmsford, Essex

6 Thursday
Chelmsford Summer Beer & Cider Festival, Chelmsford,
Essex; Scottish Real Ale Festival, Edinburgh

7 Friday
Beer on the Wye, Hereford;
Chelmsford Summer Beer & Cider Festival, Chelmsford, Essex;
Scottish Real Ale Festival, Edinburgh

8 Saturday
Beer on the Wye, Hereford;
Chelmsford Summer Beer & Cider Festival, Chelmsford, Essex;
Scottish Real Ale Festival, Edinburgh

9 Sunday   ○
Beer on the Wye, Hereford

Monday		3	10	17	24	31
Tuesday		4	11	18	25	
Wednesday		5	12	19	26	
Thursday		6	13	20	27	
Friday		7	14	21	28	
Saturday	1	8	15	22	29	
Sunday	2	9	16	23	30	

July 2017

Castelain Ch'ti Blonde (6.4%)

Brasserie Castelain, Bénifontaine

chti.com

14th July – Bastille Day

It's time for the old joke to be wheeled out, I'm afraid: 228 years ago today, the French were revolting. On 14 July the citizens of Paris finally told the King what they thought of him, and around 1,000 invaders marched on the Bastille prison. Soon the Revolution was in full steam, the guillotine slicing away the power of the royalty and the associated aristocracy, and the French republic born.

Bastille Day, as outsiders call it, or Fête National as it is known in France, was officially declared a holiday in 1880 and is still celebrated with gusto. There's a military parade up the Champs-Elysées, firework displays staged from Calais to Cannes, and a glass or two of vin dispatched as part of the fun. Even beer gets a look in, which is as it should be in a country that may major on wine but has a brewing industry that is well worth shouting about.

The heartland of French beer production is in the north of the country. Here, Castelain brewery can be found. It has been run by the same family since 1926 and markets most of its beers under the Ch'ti name, which is local slang for a northerner. Ch'ti Blonde is a glorious golden ale with a spicy, hay-like aroma. The taste is sweet, honeyed and slightly syrupy but cut through with generous carbonation and a mild herbal bitterness. It's a big satisfying beer and, because it can easily be found in generous 750ml bottles, there's enough to share on a festive day like today.

The Eiffel Tower illuminated for Bastille Day

10 Monday

14 Friday

11 Tuesday

15 Saturday

12 Wednesday

Battle of the Boyne
Public holiday Northern Ireland

16 Sunday ◑

13 Thursday

Monday		3	10	17	24	31
Tuesday		4	11	18	25	
Wednesday		5	12	19	26	
Thursday		6	13	20	27	
Friday		7	14	21	28	
Saturday	1	8	15	22	29	
Sunday	2	9	16	23	30	

Triple fff Moondance (4.2%)

The Triple fff Brewery, Alton, Hampshire

triplefff.com

Buzz Aldrin walks on the moon

20th July – The first moon landing, 1969

Well, if it was a hoax, it was a damn good one. On 20 July 1969, four days after blasting off from Cape Canaveral, Neil Armstrong and Buzz Aldrin set foot on the moon. The world watched as one, in awe of man's first steps on another galactic rock. No doubt a few beers were sunk in celebration.

There are any number of lunar-themed liquids with which you could mark the occasion, but one that takes some beating is Moondance from Triple fff, a microbrewery based near Alton in Hampshire.

A glance through Triple fff's brewing books reveals such ales as Stairway to Heaven and Dazed and Confused, both paying homage to Led Zeppelin. There's also Comfortably Numb (Pink Floyd) and Pressed Rat and Warthog, which is a track from Cream's 1968 album *Wheels of Fire*. So it seems that this Moondance would have more to do with the jaunty, jazzy track by Van Morrison than extraterrestrial activity.

The beer was one of Triple fff's early brews when it first fired up its copper in 1997. The clever blending of three hops – the solid bitterness of Northdown, the versatility of the fruity hedgerow strain First Gold and the assertive citrus notes of Cascade – has proved a winning combination. Moondance now has a couple of Champion Beer of Britain medals to its name, having won the Best Bitter category in 2002 and finishing third overall in 2006. Full and fruity, with a resonant bitterness, it's a fine way to mark any occasion – whether it actually happened or not.

17 Monday

18 Tuesday

19 Wednesday

20 Thursday
Kent Beer Festival, Canterbury, Kent

21 Friday
Kent Beer Festival, Canterbury, Kent

22 Saturday
Kent Beer Festival, Canterbury, Kent

23 Sunday ●

Monday		3	10	17	24	31
Tuesday		4	11	18	25	
Wednesday		5	12	19	26	
Thursday		6	13	20	27	
Friday		7	14	21	28	
Saturday	1	8	15	22	29	
Sunday	2	9	16	23	30	

Westerham William Wilberforce Freedom Ale (4.8%)

Westerham Brewing Co. Ltd, Edenbridge, Kent

westerhambrewery.co.uk

Stained glass window in Clapham depicting William Wilberforce

29th July – William Wilberforce dies, 1833

Robert Wicks, founder of Westerham Brewery in Kent, is a devoted Christian, and ethics play a large part in his business. To mark the 200th anniversary of the abolition of slavery in the UK, Westerham created a beer that not only recognized this landmark event but also highlighted the evil of modern-day slavery, in the form of people trafficking. Robert called the beer William Wilberforce Freedom Ale, after the man who pushed through the bill that outlawed this iniquitous practice in the early 19th century.

William Wilberforce was born in Hull in 1759, and became Member of Parliament for his home city. His political driving force turned out to be his evangelical Christianity. For 18 years, he campaigned in Parliament for the abolition of slavery, finally finding success in 1807, when the trade was outlawed. The battle was not over, however, as people already held in slavery were not immediately set free. That was eventually achieved in 1833, the year in which Wilberforce died.

William Wilberforce Freedom Ale is brewed from floor-malted Maris Otter pale malt and crystal malt, with Kentish Northdown and Golding hops providing the bitterness and balance. A high percentage of Fairtrade demerara sugar also forms part of the mix. Lively citrus fruit, gentle hop resins and light, biscuity malt fill the aroma, which is followed by full, smooth malt in the mouth, layered with tart fruit and bitter hops. The finish is dry, tangy, hoppy and notably bitter.

For every pint sold, a contribution is made to an organization called Stop the Traffik, a multinational body set up to raise public awareness of today's slave trade. Buy a bottle today and give them your support.

24 Monday

28 Friday

25 Tuesday

29 Saturday

26 Wednesday

30 Sunday ◑

27 Thursday

Monday		3	10	17	24	31
Tuesday		4	11	18	25	
Wednesday		5	12	19	26	
Thursday		6	13	20	27	
Friday		7	14	21	28	
Saturday	1	8	15	22	29	
Sunday	2	9	16	23	30	

Saltaire Challenger Special (5.2%)

Saltaire Brewery Ltd, Shipley, West Yorkshire

saltairebrewery.co.uk

The Yorkshire flag flying over Ilkley

1st August – Yorkshire Day

Is there a region of the United Kingdom that is so fiercely self-confident as Yorkshire? Yorkshire pride reaches its zenith on 1 August with Yorkshire Day, the origins of which lie in the reorganization of historic counties in 1974. Like many old parts of Britain, Yorkshire was dismembered in the local government reshuffle, and the three Ridings – North, West and East – into which it was historically divided were lost. Traditionalists loathed the idea and set up the Yorkshire Ridings Society to express their protest. The designation of a Yorkshire Day, starting in 1975, was one means of publicising their unhappiness. The date of 1 August was chosen because it was on this day in 1759 that Yorkshire soldiers, leaving the Battle of Minden in Germany, stopped and collected white roses as a tribute to their fallen colleagues. The white rose has remained the county's emblem ever since.

Yorkshire ale is also rather special. Today I've opted for one of the excellent beers from Saltaire Brewery, based in an old power station in Shipley, just north of Bradford. Any of their fine ales would do but, if it's available, it's worth checking out Challenger Special, which, like all Saltaire's beers, does what it says on the label, in true, plain-speaking Yorkshire fashion.

Challenger is the main hop in this special ale, with Fuggle in support. The grist is comprised of pale malt and dark crystal malt, with some crystal rye and roasted barley, which immediately suggests that this is going to have a rich, nutty character. That's what emerges in the taste, with hints of liquorice, molasses and tropical fruit, all excellently balanced by bitterness from both the roasted grain and the generous hopping. It's a robust, forthright, good-value beer – a fine, beery manifestation, perhaps, of the proud and defiant Yorkshire temperament.

31 Monday

1 Tuesday

2 Wednesday

3 Thursday
Worcester Beer, Cider & Perry Festival, Worcester

4 Friday
Worcester Beer, Cider & Perry Festival, Worcester

5 Saturday
Worcester Beer, Cider & Perry Festival, Worcester

6 Sunday

Monday	31	7	14	21	28
Tuesday	1	8	15	22	29
Wednesday	2	9	16	23	30
Thursday	3	10	17	24	31
Friday	4	11	18	25	
Saturday	5	12	19	26	
Sunday	6	13	20	27	

Left Hand Good Juju (4.5%)

Left Hand Brewing Co., Longmont, Colorado

lefthandbrewing.com

13th August – International Left-Hander's Day

It's a club with an illustrious membership list. US Presidents Gerald Ford, Ronald Reagan, George Bush and Bill Clinton; Queen Victoria, Prince Charles and Prince William; Lewis Carroll, Mark Twain and HG Wells; Leonardo da Vinci, Michelangelo and Raphael. The organization in question is The Left-Handers Club, formed in 1990 to provide a voice for the 10%, or thereabouts, of the world's population that is left-handed. As part of its remit, it raises awareness with Left-Handers' Day, which falls on 13 August.

We can do our bit for the cause by choosing a beer from the Left Hand Brewing Company. The name was derived from an Arapahoe Indian chief whose tribe used to winter in the area local to the brewery. His name was Niwot, meaning Left Hand.

One of the company's earliest creations is something out of the ordinary, as left-handers may well consider themselves to be. The defining feature is the inclusion of crushed fresh ginger root. The taste is crisp, clean and pleasantly bitter. There's a hoppy edge and, of course, a warming bite of ginger, but it's all deftly done so that the ginger is subtle and supportive rather than bold and boisterous. The spice comes through yet again in the dry and bitter finish, making it mildly warming. Raise the glass in your left hand and enjoy.

7 Monday
Public holiday Scotland

○

8 Tuesday
Great British Beer Festival, Olympia, London

9 Wednesday
Great British Beer Festival, Olympia, London

10 Thursday
Great British Beer Festival, Olympia, London

11 Friday
Great British Beer Festival, Olympia, London

12 Saturday
Great British Beer Festival, Olympia, London

13 Sunday

Monday		7	14	21	28
Tuesday	1	8	15	22	29
Wednesday	2	9	16	23	30
Thursday	3	10	17	24	31
Friday	4	11	18	25	
Saturday	5	12	19	26	
Sunday	6	13	20	27	

Duvel Moortgat **Duvel** (8.5%)

Brouwerij Moortgat, Breendonk-Puurs

duvel.be

14th August – St Arnold of Soissons's Day

St Arnold of Soissons is celebrated as the patron saint of Belgian brewers. He retired from the bishopric of Soissons, to set up his own abbey in Oudenburg, Flanders. The Belgians need little excuse to quaff a beer or two, and perhaps Arnold was partly responsible for this admirable affection for ale. Recognizing that beer was far safer to drink than untreated water, he advised his flock to make it their daily tipple. He wouldn't have known that it was the boiling part of the brewing process that made beer so healthy by killing off most of the germs, but he did know that fewer people died after drinking beer than drinking the fetid local water.

It seems a touch blasphemous to celebrate a saint's day with a devil of a beer, but one would hope that Arnold wouldn't mind that much, considering it still keeps Flemish folk off the water. Duvel ('Devil' in Dutch) is one of Belgium's best-known beery exports. It's also a trendsetter. The Moortgat brewery at Puurs, just south of Antwerp, coined a new beer style when it created this pale golden beer at the end of the 1960s. The use of a Scottish ale yeast provided a novel twist, enhanced by a delicate hopping from Czech Saaz and Slovenian Styrian Goldings. It proved that beer didn't have to be dark to be packed with flavour. The light body and zesty fruitiness, with more than a touch of pear, really make it dangerously drinkable for its strength. It's not called Devil for nothing.

14 Monday

15 Tuesday ☽

16 Wednesday

17 Thursday

18 Friday

19 Saturday

20 Sunday

Monday		7	14	21	28
Tuesday	1	8	15	22	29
Wednesday	2	9	16	23	30
Thursday	3	10	17	24	31
Friday	4	11	18	25	
Saturday	**5**	**12**	**19**	**26**	
Sunday	**6**	**13**	**20**	**27**	

Black Wolf William Wallace (4.5%)

Black Wolf Brewery, Stirling

blackwolfbrewery.com

23rd August – William Wallace dies, 1305

Black Wolf operates from a brewhouse in Stirling. It specializes in beers that glorify the proud history of Scotland, one of which is the obvious choice for 23 August – the day that freedom fighter William Wallace met a bloody end at the hands of his mortal enemies, the English.

Wallace was born around 1270, most likely in Renfrewshire. He gained a reputation as a rebel when he struck out against the bullying English, who had taken over Scotland in 1296 and imposed unpopular high taxes. He was one of the leaders of the Scottish uprising against King Edward I, and triumphed at the Battle of Stirling Bridge later the same year. However, the English were not beaten, and rallied to inflict a revenge defeat at the Battle of Falkirk in 1298. Following the defeat, Wallace refused to bend to English rule. Thus he became known as an outlaw and a traitor, and, when captured near Glasgow in 1305, he was taken to London for a show trial. There, in the absence of defence lawyers and even a jury, he was sentenced to death.

The copper-coloured beer that Black Wolf brews in his memory has a distinctly Scottish accent, in the form of a dominant malty presence. It was first brewed in 2006 and is derived from a malt grist of pale, crystal, chocolate and caramalt, with a little wheat. First Gold hops are used for both bitterness and aroma.

There are hints of chocolate in the nutty aroma, while the taste is bittersweet and crisp. The finish, meanwhile, is dry, malty, nutty and enjoyably bitter.

Statue of William Wallace near Dryburgh

21 Monday ●

25 Friday

Peterborough Beer Festival,
Peterborough, Cambridgeshire

22 Tuesday

Peterborough Beer Festival,
Peterborough, Cambridgeshire

26 Saturday

Peterborough Beer Festival,
Peterborough, Cambridgeshire

23 Wednesday

Peterborough Beer Festival,
Peterborough, Cambridgeshire

27 Sunday

24 Thursday

Peterborough Beer Festival,
Peterborough, Cambridgeshire

Monday		7	14	21	28
Tuesday	1	8	15	22	29
Wednesday	2	9	16	23	30
Thursday	3	10	17	24	31
Friday	4	11	18	25	
Saturday	5	12	19	26	
Sunday	6	13	20	27	

August/September 2017

Hopdaemon Leviathan (6%)

Hopdaemon Brewery Co., Newnham, Kent

hopdaemon.com

Morris dancers at the Faversham Hop Festival

2nd September – Faversham Hop Festival

Offer most people today the chance of a back-breaking 'holiday' in Kent, bringing in the hop harvest, and they'll laugh in your face. Yet, until the days of mechanization, the chance of a month in the fresh, country air was too good to refuse for the working classes trapped in the smoggy streets of London. Whole families set up temporary home in the farmland camps, working together from dawn till dusk, plucking the hop flowers from the bines.

With the arrival of mechanical hop picking in the 1950s, the annual Cockney invasion came to an end. However, its legacy is still celebrated in an annual festival staged at Faversham, usually over the first weekend in September. Launched in 1991, this is an opportunity to revisit the boisterous spirit of the hop-picking days, with singing, dancing, street entertainers, musicians, a 'hoppers' ball' and, of course, gallons of Kentish ale.

A Kentish brewery making good use of hops is Hopdaemon, founded by New Zealander Tonie Prins. His Leviathan, is a 6% 'beast of a beer'. The malt grist is complex, packed with pale, crystal, chocolate and caramalt varieties, plus a little wheat malt, with Fuggle and Bramling Cross hops working their magic in the copper. The beer glows red in colour, and has hints of pineapple and lemon showing through the dark malt in the nose. Juicy, fruity hops skip and jump over the palate, merging with estery fermentation flavours to provide pineapple and pepper notes that offset the smooth sweet malt. The dry finish is fruity and hoppy, too.

28 Monday

Public holiday England, Wales & Northern Ireland

1 Friday

29 Tuesday ☽

2 Saturday

Eid-al-Adah

30 Wednesday

3 Sunday

31 Thursday

Monday		7	14	21	28
Tuesday	1	8	15	22	29
Wednesday	2	9	16	23	30
Thursday	3	10	17	24	31
Friday	4	11	18	25	1
Saturday	5	12	19	26	2
Sunday	6	13	20	27	3

Wolf Granny Wouldn't Like It!!! (4.8%)

The Wolf Brewery, Besthorpe, Norfolk

wolfbrewery.com

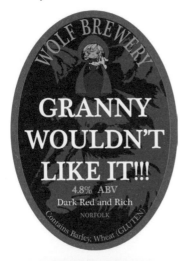

10th September – Grandparents' Day

On the face of it, today's celebration is just another schmaltzy American creation, something that's not even noted on this side of the Atlantic. Grandparents' Day, however, does have a moral root, as its founder, West Virginian housewife Marian McQuade, explained when she started campaigning for it back in 1970.

To Mrs McQuade, the neglect by young people of the wisdom and knowledge of their elderly relatives was a crime. McQuade took her proposal for a Grandparents' Day to the West Virginia state government with rapid success, and within eight years President Jimmy Carter signed an annual Grandparents' Day celebration into law.

As a bit of fun for the occasion, you could send your grandmother a bottle of beer from Wolf Brewery. The beer highlighted for today is called Granny Wouldn't Like It!!!, but it would be worth seeing if she did.

The pump clip depicts Little Red Riding Hood, however, fairy tale artwork and a gimmicky name do little to reflect the interesting profile of this amber-red strong ale. With pale, crystal, chocolate and wheat malts in the mash tun, there's plenty of body to this beer, providing roasted notes in the taste and finish, while Golding and Challenger hops supply a peppery balance and some vinous fruit.

If Granny doesn't like it after all, then give it to Grandad, who will be sure to tell you all about the beers he enjoyed when he was a lad. You see: the grey generation do have important things to pass on.

Grandparents' Day is a celebration of the wisdom of older generations

4 Monday

8 Friday

Chappel Beer Festival, Chappel, Essex

5 Tuesday

Chappel Beer Festival, Chappel, Essex

9 Saturday

Chappel Beer Festival, Chappel, Essex

6 Wednesday   ○

Chappel Beer Festival, Chappel, Essex

10 Sunday

7 Thursday

Chappel Beer Festival, Chappel, Essex

Monday		4	11	18	25
Tuesday		5	12	19	26
Wednesday		6	13	20	27
Thursday		7	14	21	28
Friday	1	8	15	22	29
Saturday	2	9	16	23	30
Sunday	3	10	17	24	

Silenrieux Joseph (5.4%)

Brasserie de Silenrieux, Silenrieux

www.brasseriedesilenrieux.be

17th September – Hildegard of Bingen dies, 1179

Brewers latch onto patron saints with unseemly eagerness. Perhaps it is the suggestion of vice that hangs around their product that prompts them to look for a holy sponsor. Today's saint in question is Hildegard of Bingen, who was born in the year 1098 and sent to a convent at the age of eight. Thereafter, she dedicated her whole life to the church as an abbess in the Benedictine order, gaining a reputation as a great healer and source of wisdom.

The importance of Hildegard for brewers lies in the fact that she encouraged her followers to drink beer, realizing that it was safer than polluted water, and also because she was the first person to extol the use of hops in beer. This was all part of Hildegard's promotion of a balanced lifestyle and a healthy diet.

Interestingly, one food product that she advocated strongly was spelt. This cousin of wheat can be used for making beer, and one of the best beers to be based on it comes from the Silenrieux brewery in Belgium. Joseph is a witbier-style beer, typically hazy yellow in the glass, and including spices instead of hoppiness for balance. The aroma presents sweet and sour lemons, spices and a faintly nutty, bready cereal note. In the mouth, the beer is lively and refreshingly bittersweet, with spritzy citrus notes, a soft dryness and gentle herbs. Once again, nutty cereals – no doubt the spelt showing through – provide a light backdrop. It's a clean and classy, bottle-conditioned beer that retains your interest right through to the bittersweet, slightly chewy, faintly nutty, drying finish in which sweet lemon flavours linger.

You have to be careful about labelling a beer as a health drink but, as this one draws together two nutritious foods that she rated highly, the wise Hildegard would surely have nodded her approval to Joseph.

11 Monday

12 Tuesday

13 Wednesday ☽

14 Thursday
York Beer & Cider Festival, York

15 Friday
York Beer & Cider Festival, York;
Poperinge Beer and Hop Festival, Poperinge, Belgium

16 Saturday
York Beer & Cider Festival, York;
Oktoberfest, Munich, Germany;
Poperinge Beer and Hop Festival, Poperinge, Belgium

17 Sunday
York Beer & Cider Festival, York;
Oktoberfest, Munich, Germany;
Poperinge Beer and Hop Festival, Poperinge, Belgium

Monday		4	11	18	25
Tuesday		5	12	19	26
Wednesday		6	13	20	27
Thursday		7	14	21	28
Friday	1	8	15	22	29
Saturday	2	9	16	23	30
Sunday	3	10	17	24	

Huyghe Delirium Tremens (8.5%)

Brouwerij Huyghe, Melle

delirium.be

Elephant family in the Maasai Mara

22nd September – Elephant Appreciation Day

It seems at first glance like just another of those Internet-promoted non-events – but Elephant Appreciation Day is now being exploited for more important, conservation reasons. Wayne Hepburn launched the first Elephant Appreciation Day in 1996 because, among other things, the elephant 'is most undeservedly threatened with extinction' and 'is entertaining and amusing'. The initiative has been latched on to by charities such as America's In Defense of Animals, which is using 22 September to ask the public to consider the fate of maltreated elephants.

You could ponder the fate of this noble beast with a glass of a Belgian beer that also sees the elephant as a fun figure. The beer is called Delirium Tremens, and on the label you'll find little pink elephants, the unwritten message being that if you drink too much of a beer as strong as this (8.5%), then don't be surprised if you start seeing strange things. It's all very odd really because this is a seriously good beer. It has complex estery fruit in the nose – banana, peach and pear – over creamy pale malt. Considering its potency, it's frighteningly easy to drink, a bittersweet, fruity, citrus-sharp, golden ale with a light spiciness, an airy texture and a clean balance of flavours. Not surprisingly, the finish is warming with a bitter fruit character.

The beer is described as 'triple fermented', and is the result of the action of three different yeasts. It was created on Boxing Day 1989, which seems as good a day as any to come up with a beer that derives its name from the after-effects of over-indulgence. In pachyderm terminology, it's the sort of beer that, once tasted, you never forget.

18 Monday

Oktoberfest, Munich, Germany

22 Friday

Oktoberfest, Munich, Germany;
Autumn equinox, Islamic New Year

19 Tuesday

Oktoberfest, Munich, Germany

23 Saturday

Oktoberfest, Munich, Germany

20 Wednesday ●

Oktoberfest, Munich, Germany

24 Sunday

Oktoberfest, Munich, Germany

21 Thursday

Oktoberfest, Munich, Germany;
Rosh Hashana

Monday		4	11	18	25
Tuesday		5	12	19	26
Wednesday		6	13	20	27
Thursday		7	14	21	28
Friday	1	8	15	22	29
Saturday	2	9	16	23	30
Sunday	3	10	17	24	

Samuel Adams Triple Bock (18%)

The Boston Beer Co., Boston, Massachusetts

samueladams.com

27th September – Samuel Adams born, 1722

America's most successful craft brewery is called The Boston Beer Company. Most people don't know it by that name, however. They just call it Samuel Adams. Boston Beer was founded by Jim Koch in 1984. His first brew was an immediate smash. He named the beer Samuel Adams Boston Lager, latching on to a famous figure in American history.

Samuel Adams was himself born into a brewing family, but he made his name as a politician and patriot, a man who roused public sentiment against the insensitive British. He was one of the founders of the rebellious group behind the act of defiance that became known as the Boston Tea Party. Adams emerged onto the national stage and was one of the signatories of the American Declaration of Independence in 1776. He served as Governor of Massachusetts between 1793 and 1797, and died in 1803.

The name of Samuel Adams has since been extended across Boston Beer's range of products, including to the occasionally-brewed beer selected for today. The brewery claims that Triple Bock 'stretches the definition of beer'. It emerges from the bottle at a whopping 18% ABV. It is brewed from pale and caramel malts, German Tettnang hops and a little maple syrup, and then matured in oak whiskey barrels. The nose is immediately heady, alcoholic, oaky, malty and laced with dried fruits such as raisins and sultanas. It's spicy, too, with traces of treacle, liquorice and even Marmite. On the palate, Triple Bock has virtually no carbonation, giving a soft, silky mouthfeel as a backdrop to sweet caramel, creamy dried fruit, a peppery warmth, soft powdery chocolate and a bitter, cedary note. Elements of all the above linger on into the warming finish, but basically every sip unearths something new.

September/October 25–1

25 Monday
Oktoberfest, Munich, Germany

26 Tuesday
Oktoberfest, Munich, Germany

27 Wednesday
Oktoberfest, Munich, Germany;
St Albans Beer & Cider Festival, St Albans, Hertfordshire

28 Thursday
Oktoberfest, Munich, Germany;
St Albans Beer & Cider Festival, St Albans, Hertfordshire

29 Friday
Oktoberfest, Munich, Germany;
St Albans Beer & Cider Festival, St Albans, Hertfordshire

30 Saturday
Oktoberfest, Munich, Germany;
St Albans Beer & Cider Festival, St Albans, Hertfordshire;
Yom Kippur

1 Sunday
Oktoberfest, Munich, Germany

Monday		4	11	18	25
Tuesday		5	12	19	26
Wednesday		6	13	20	27
Thursday		7	14	21	28
Friday	1	8	15	22	29
Saturday	2	9	16	23	30
Sunday	3	10	17	24	1

Budweiser Budvar (5%)

Budějovický Budvar, n.p., České Budějovice

budvar.cz

7th October – First beer brewed at Budweiser Budvar, 1895

České Budějovice is a town in the south of the Czech Republic, not far from the Austrian border. In the 19th century, it was heavily populated by Germans and seen very much as a German town. The town name was even known by its German title, Budweis – hence the origin of the term Budweiser, meaning 'from the town of Budweis'.

By the end of the 19th century, however, the Czechs began to fight back. Deprived of a significant voice in local politics they recognized the need for more financial and commercial muscle to challenge the unfair status quo, and Czech banks and factories were founded to rival dominant German concerns. An obvious progression – for a country where beer was an important part of everyday life – was to establish a Czech brewery. So it was that the Czech Joint Stock Brewery was formed, taking investment from Czech citizens and building on assurances from the Czech-owned bars and restaurants that they would take the new beer in preference to the German alternative, as long as it was of good quality.

They weren't to be disappointed. On 7 October 1895, the first beer was brewed at what has now become known as Budweiser Budvar. To ensure the beer was of top quality when it went on sale, it underwent a long period of maturation after fermentation. Not a drop reached the outside world until Christmas. So Budvar was born and with it its now-famous reputation for extensive conditioning.

Today, Budvar is still cold-conditioned, in fact for a full 90 days – a lagering period that rounds off all the rough edges and produces one of the world's smoothest and best-balanced beers. Other Czech breweries have changed their methods of fermentation and cut down the conditioning time, but Budvar makes great play of its adherence to tradition. The long-awaited result is a delicate balance of ripe sweet malt and gently tangy hops, with a herbal, vanilla-like finish that defines the Budweiser drinking experience.

Coppers at the Budweiser Budvar brewery

2 Monday
Oktoberfest, Munich, Germany

3 Tuesday
Oktoberfest, Munich, Germany

4 Wednesday

5 Thursday   ○
Great American Beer Festival, Denver, Colorado, USA

6 Friday
Ascot Beer Festival, Ascot, Berkshire;
Great American Beer Festival, Denver, Colorado, USA

7 Saturday
Ascot Beer Festival, Ascot, Berkshire;
Great American Beer Festival, Denver, Colorado, USA

8 Sunday

Monday		2	9	16	23	30
Tuesday		3	10	17	24	31
Wednesday		4	11	18	25	
Thursday		5	12	19	26	
Friday		6	13	20	27	
Saturday		7	14	21	28	
Sunday	1	8	15	22	29	

Cottage Norman's Conquest (7%)

Cottage Brewing Co., Lovington, Somerset

www.cottagebrewing.co.uk

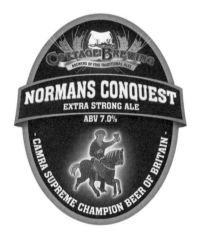

14th October – Battle of Hastings, 1066

The Battle of Hastings on this day in 1066 was the culmination of William of Normandy's long-planned invasion of England. His objective was to take the crown, a title once possibly promised him by his cousin, King Edward the Confessor, but one that had in the meantime passed to Harold, Earl of Wessex. William invaded the south coast and raided local settlements to draw Harold into a fight, the two armies squaring up on a field just outside the town of Hastings.

At first, the battle seemed to go Harold's way. His men repelled assault after assault from the Normans. Eventually, however, the numbers took their toll and the English were overrun. Harold, as depicted in the illustration of the battle on the Bayeux Tapestry, took an arrow in the eye and was then mown down. William claimed the battle and with it the English throne.

Cottage Brewery's Norman's Conquest takes its name from the brewery founder, Chris Norman, but it depicts a character, possibly a refugee from the Bayeux Tapestry, on its label. Also appropriate to the beer's identity is its original gravity – the reading taken before fermentation begins, which tells the brewer how much sugar there is in the wort – which, in this case, is 1066. When brewed out, this brings the beer up to a formidable 7% ABV. This rich, dark ale has a vinous fruitiness and sweetish, roasted malt flavours that linger on in the finish – all skilfully conjured out of a mix of pale, crystal and chocolate malts, spiced with Challenger hops.

The Bayeux Tapestry

9 Monday

13 Friday

Robin Hood Beer Festival, Nottingham

10 Tuesday

14 Saturday

Robin Hood Beer Festival, Nottingham

11 Wednesday

Robin Hood Beer Festival, Nottingham

15 Sunday

12 Thursday ☽

Robin Hood Beer Festival, Nottingham

Monday		2	9	16	23	30
Tuesday		3	10	17	24	31
Wednesday		4	11	18	25	
Thursday		5	12	19	26	
Friday		6	13	20	27	
Saturday		7	14	21	28	
Sunday	1	8	15	22	29	

Mighty Oak Oscar Wilde (3.7%)

Mighty Oak Brewing Company, Maldon, Essex

mightyoakbrewery.co.uk

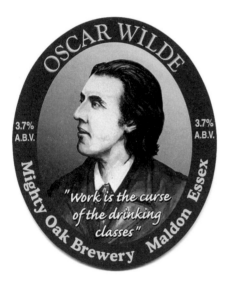

16th October – Oscar Wilde born, 1854

The world of literature is well endowed with flamboyant, eccentric characters, and one of the most outrageous entered the world on this day in 1854.

Oscar Wilde is best known for his literary works: the novel *The Picture of Dorian Gray*, the plays *Lady Windermere's Fan* and *The Importance of Being Earnest*, and the poem 'The Ballad of Reading Gaol', which was written after a two-year incarceration (with hard labour) for homosexual activity. Wilde had been a true celebrity of his era, a reckless non-conformist in prim-and-proper times, but he never recovered his earlier social acceptance after his time in prison. On release, he moved to Paris, adopting a pseudonym, and there he died, three years later, in 1900.

The other thing that Wilde has become famous for is his acerbic wit. 'Work is the curse of the drinking classes', he once quipped, and these words now appear on the pump clip of a beer that also shares his name from the Mighty Oak brewery in Maldon, Essex. Oscar Wilde Mild was first brewed in 1999 and soon became part of the regular range. Pale, crystal and black malts combine to provide a deep mahogany colour with red highlights, a soft mouthfeel and a pleasant coffee accent to the nose, taste and drying finish, with bittersweet notes encouraged by the presence of Challenger hops.

'Moderation is a fatal thing – nothing succeeds like excess,' Wilde once jested. I would never suggest taking that approach with beer, but it's certainly tempting with a brew like this.

October 16–22

16 Monday

17 Tuesday

18 Wednesday

19 Thursday ●

20 Friday

21 Saturday

22 Sunday

Monday		2	9	16	23	30
Tuesday		3	10	17	24	31
Wednesday		4	11	18	25	
Thursday		5	12	19	26	
Friday		6	13	20	27	
Saturday		7	14	21	28	
Sunday	1	8	15	22	29	

97

Samuel Adams Black Lager (4.9%)

The Boston Beer Co., Boston, Massachusetts

samueladams.com

24th October – Black Thursday, 1929

Thursday 24 October 1929 was a disastrous day for the American economy. In the post World War I years, America – to borrow a phrase coined later by Harold Macmillan – had never had it so good: US businesses were booming, dividends rose steadily and share prices climbed accordingly. It seemed that there could be no end to the nation's increasing prosperity.

All this optimism came to a sudden and abrupt halt on this day in 1929. The day began with share disposals on the New York Stock Exchange that turned into panic selling when the tickertape system for recording prices fell an hour and a half behind. In a normal day, the stock exchange would have expected around four million transactions; on what became known as Black Thursday, there were nearly 13 million. The ensuing panic saw US share prices plummet, and all confidence in the financial markets disappeared. Fortunes were lost, and America collapsed into depression, with unemployment at record levels.

It's not a particularly cheerful day to celebrate. But we can make it a bit brighter with an American beer that may be equally dark in nature but is always an uplifting experience.

First brewed in 2004 in the tradition of the East German schwarzbier, Samuel Adams Black Lager includes Munich malt plus a trademarked, husk-free German malt called Carafa, that ensures the beer doesn't become too dry. The name says black but the beer pours a deep ruby-red. Biscuity chocolate notes fill the aroma and continue into the bittersweet, nutty, caramel-accented taste and the drying finish. The hopping, with German Spalt and Hallertauer Mittelfrüh, is light. Beers like this work well because they provide all the dark malt flavours of a stout combined with the crispness and cleanness of a well-lagered beer. This one also proves that you can have a Black Thursday without getting depressed.

Crowds of people gathered outside the New York Stock Exchange

23 Monday

27 Friday ☽

24 Tuesday

28 Saturday

25 Wednesday

29 Sunday
Daylight Saving Time ends

26 Thursday

Monday		2	9	16	23	30
Tuesday		3	10	17	24	31
Wednesday		4	11	18	25	
Thursday		5	12	19	26	
Friday		6	13	20	27	
Saturday		7	14	21	28	
Sunday	1	8	15	22	29	

Harvey's Bonfire Boy (5.8%)

Harvey & Son, Lewes, East Sussex

harveysonline.co.uk

Guy Fawkes effigy at the Lewes Bonfire Night procession

5th November – Gunpowder plot

The story behind the infamous Gunpowder Plot needs little explanation here. A group of Catholic conspirators tried to blow up the Houses of Parliament during their state opening by the religiously suppressive King James I. Guido 'Guy' Fawkes, was caught red-handed with the explosives. Imprisoned in the Tower of London, Fawkes was tortured into confession and executed by hanging, drawing and quartering. When bonfire celebrations began a year later, on the orders of King James, it was an effigy of the Pope that sat atop the rising flames. Since the 19th century, the Pope has been tactfully replaced with a dummy of Fawkes.

There is nowhere in Britain where bonfire celebrations are more elaborate than at Lewes in East Sussex. This historic market town has been marking the foiling of the Gunpowder Plot for more than 150 years in dramatic style, and still burns an effigy of 16th-century Pope Paul V alongside the familiar 'guy'. Six bonfire societies host the event, arranging barrel racing down the high street, torch-lit, costumed processions and a flurry of fireworks.

Marking the event is a beer from the town's brewery. Harvey's Bonfire Boy is a strong, malty, warming ale that really hits the spot at this time of year. It is brewed from a grist of Maris Otter pale malt, crystal malt and black malt, with four types of hops – Fuggle, Golding, Progress and Bramling Cross – for balance. The abundant malt shows its presence in a sugary sweet taste balanced by the bitter, smoky notes of roasted grain. To add a further dimension, zesty orange notes bounce around the palate, dodging light alcohol vapours like a jumping jack, and there are pruney dried fruit notes, too. When it comes to the finish, the sweetness persists but hops fight their way through as the beer begins to dry.

30 Monday

31 Tuesday
Halloween

1 Wednesday
All Saints' Day

2 Thursday
All Souls' Day

3 Friday

4 Saturday ○

5 Sunday
Guy Fawkes Day

Monday	30	6	13	20	27
Tuesday	31	7	14	21	28
Wednesday	1	8	15	22	29
Thursday	2	9	16	23	30
Friday	3	10	17	24	
Saturday	4	11	18	25	
Sunday	5	12	19	26	

November 2017

Otley O8 (8%)

Otley Brewing Company, Pontypridd, Glamorgan

otleybrewing.co.uk

Poet Dylan Thomas

9th November – Dylan Thomas dies, 1953

Has there ever been a better description of the joys of drinking beer than that delivered by Dylan Thomas in his short story 'Old Garbo'? You can almost savour the ale with him as he revels in the glory of a good pint.

'I liked the taste of the beer,' he says, 'its live, white lather, its brass-bright depth, the sudden world through the wet brown walls of the glass, the tilted rush to the lips and the slow swallowing down to the lapping belly, the salt on the tongue, the foam at the corners.'

Thomas was born in Swansea in 1914. His first book of poetry was published in 1934, and he headed for London in the same year, beginning work for the BBC as a writer of documentaries. Vibrant prose and dramatic works ensued, as did performances in front of the microphone as a radio actor, and a pint glass was rarely far from his lips. From first-hand accounts, Thomas was a showman, taking advantage of the glow gleaned from a few beers to warm to his pub audience.

If the life of someone so naturally gifted is to be toasted, it cannot be with anything other than beer, and good beer at that, which is why today's bibulous offering is a former CAMRA Champion Beer of Wales.

Otley Brewery's O8 is a fruity, 8% barley wine, packing sweet sultana and earthy hop resin flavours, with a lingering orange note in the finish, courtesy of Progress and Bramling Cross hops. I can't get anywhere close to the poetry in Dylan Thomas's words when it comes to describing such a beer, so I'll leave you to seek out a pint or a bottle and let the muse of beer speak for itself.

6 Monday

10 Friday ◐

7 Tuesday

11 Saturday
Remembrance Day

8 Wednesday

12 Sunday
Remembrance Sunday

9 Thursday

Monday		6	13	20	27
Tuesday		7	14	21	28
Wednesday	1	8	15	22	29
Thursday	2	9	16	23	30
Friday	3	10	17	24	
Saturday	4	11	18	25	
Sunday	5	12	19	26	

Hofbräu Edelweiss Weissbier (5.3%)

Brau Union, Austria

edelweissbier.at

Julie Andrews in *The Sound of Music* film

16th November – *The Sound of Music* premieres on Broadway, 1959

On this day, Rodgers and Hammerstein's musical *The Sound of Music* enjoyed its premiere. The audience enjoyed it so much that it ran for 1,443 performances before transferring to the big screen, where it was a box office smash. Its fans never tire of the tuneful tale of a wayward nun who becomes governess to a large, unruly family, teaches them all to sing and warms the heart of their icy father. Throw in some stunning shots of alpine meadows, add a little Nazi menace, and the story was always likely to be a hit.

One of the songs gives us our lead for a beer for today. Edelweiss is an ode to the little white alpine flower of the same name, the national flower of Austria. Don't ask Austrians to sing it to you, though: the film wasn't even shown in the country's cinemas, and although Edelweiss has the air of an old alpine folk song, it was actually a new composition for the musical.

There is one Edelweiss that the Austrians know rather well, however, and do appreciate. It's a wheat beer originally from the Hofbräu Kaltenhausen brewery, the oldest brewery in the Salzburg area, with origins dating back to the 15th century. Edelweiss is presented cloudy and yellow in colour, with a big, rocky foam head, thanks to its lively carbonation. The spicy aroma offers a distinct tinned pears note, and the same fruit pushes through in the taste, which is refreshingly tart and spiked with a little herbal/clove bitterness. There are more pears in the drying, bready, herbal finish. Beerwise, when I'm thirsty, it's one of my favourite things.

13 Monday

17 Friday

14 Tuesday

18 Saturday ●

15 Wednesday

19 Sunday

16 Thursday

Monday		6	13	20	27
Tuesday		7	14	21	28
Wednesday	1	8	15	22	29
Thursday	2	9	16	23	30
Friday	3	10	17	24	
Saturday	4	11	18	25	
Sunday	5	12	19	26	

Deschutes The Abyss (11%)

Deschutes Brewery, Bend, Oregon

deschutesbrewery.com

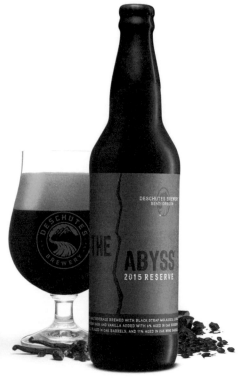

23rd November – Thanksgiving

We can't let Thanksgiving pass without finding an outstanding American beer with which to mark this historic festival. The first Thanksgiving is said to have taken place in 1621, when settlers from the Mayflower joined with local native Americans to give thanks for their first harvest. The concept evolved over time and was formally installed in the calendar by President Lincoln in 1863. These days the occasion is celebrated on the fourth Thursday of November and is as important a holiday in the US as Christmas.

An excellent beer to toast the occasion with comes from Deschutes Brewery in Bend, Oregon. They've gained a fine reputation over the years for their excellent bottled beers, but today's selection moves them into a new league. The Abyss is an imperial stout but one that has had a few twists and turns added during the production process to create a beer of remarkable character. The key twist is the ageing in French oak and Bourbon casks, which adds astonishing complexity.

The Abyss lives up to its name with broodingly dark brown appearance in the glass, topped by a lively foam the colour of a smoky bar-room ceiling. The nose is biscuity, slightly vinous and packed with the aromas of chocolate, orange and liquorice. Then there's the taste, loaded with oily chocolate flavours, nuts, coffee, hints of orange cream, a tinge of liquorice and an oaky dryness. It's super-smooth, with the sumptuousness of a chocolate truffle, only more bitter. There's more dark chocolate, coffee and oak in the warming, drying finish that follows, but you could drink this beer all night (slowly!) and keep finding new flavours. I can't think of a better way to round off a Thanksgiving meal, perhaps sipped sagely with a slice of traditional pumpkin pie.

20 Monday

21 Tuesday

22 Wednesday

23 Thursday
Thanksgiving

24 Friday

25 Saturday

26 Sunday ◐

Monday		6	13	20	27
Tuesday		7	14	21	28
Wednesday	1	8	15	22	29
Thursday	2	9	16	23	30
Friday	3	10	17	24	
Saturday	4	11	18	25	
Sunday	5	12	19	26	

Belhaven St Andrew's Ale (4.6%)

Belhaven Brewery, Dunbar, East Lothian

belhaven.co.uk

30th November – St Andrew's Day

'Homage to the home of golf from the home of good beer,' once declared the Belhaven website about St Andrew's Ale. The image that they've built around this beer suggests that the inspiration was the championship golf course on the Scottish coast, but surely at the outset it must have been Scotland's patron saint – whose feast day falls on 30 November – who gave rise to this beer?

St Andrew is one of the better-known saints, given the fact that he was one of Christ's original 12 disciples. As with many early Christian leaders, he paid a cruel price for his steadfastness in his faith and his missionary work. He was executed at Patras, Greece, crucified on an X-shaped cross, an echo of which can be found in the saltire cross that graces the flag of Scotland, one of the countries of which he is patron. It is said that the saint chose this unusual-shaped cross as he didn't consider himself worthy of the same execution as Christ.

Helping Scots celebrate the memory of their patron saint, St Andrew's Ale is brewed from pale malt, crystal malt and just a hint of black malt for colour. The hops are Challenger for bitterness and Golding added late for aroma. The result is a nicely balanced beer with a copper hue that has rich malt and sultana fruitiness in the aroma. Creamy malt and dried fruits continue in the bittersweet taste, which also has a light citrus tingle, before roasted malt comes through early in the drying, hoppy finish.

27 Monday

1 Friday

28 Tuesday

2 Saturday

29 Wednesday

3 Sunday ○

30 Thursday

St Andrew's Day
Public holiday Scotland

Monday		6	13	20	27
Tuesday		7	14	21	28
Wednesday	1	8	15	22	29
Thursday	2	9	16	23	30
Friday	3	10	17	24	*1*
Saturday	4	11	18	25	*2*
Sunday	5	12	19	26	*3*

Sierra Nevada Celebration Ale (6.8%)

Sierra Nevada Brewing Co., Chico, California

sierranevada.com

5th December – Prohibition ends in the US, 1933

5 December 1933 was a big day for American beer lovers. This was the date that the 21st amendment to the US Constitution was ratified, thereby bringing an end to the ghastly period of Prohibition. After nearly 14 years, it was once again legal to produce, sell and buy beer.

From the time the US legislature ratified the 18th Amendment in 1919, rendering the manufacture, sale or transportation of intoxicating liquors, within, into or out of the country a criminal offence, America's brewers ran into a wall. And while once-legal, commercial brewers twiddled their thumbs, illegal home-brewers, smugglers and racketeers had a field day. However, with the depression of the late 1920s gathering speed, the country grew tired of deprivation, crime and unemployment. Franklin D Roosevelt won a landslide presidential election victory on a ticket that promised the repeal of Prohibition. By the end of 1933, America was mostly wet again. Nevertheless, the devastation of the US brewing industry was obvious. Before Prohibition, the US could boast 1,568 brewers; on resumption of legal brewing, the initial number of companies able to pick up production was a mere 31, growing to 756 within a year.

For a beer to celebrate this momentous day I recommend Sierra Nevada's Celebration Ale. It's a fine example of the balanced use of pungent American hops. There are three types in all, the three Cs: Chinook, Centennial and Cascade. The result is a beer brim-full of grapefruit notes that are kept in balance by the sort of full maltiness you need to bring a beer up to 6.8%. Had it been around 80-odd years ago, it would, in itself, have been a good enough reason to repeal Prohibition.

4 Monday

8 Friday
Pigs Ear Beer & Cider Festival, Hackney, London

5 Tuesday
Pigs Ear Beer & Cider Festival, Hackney, London

9 Saturday
Pigs Ear Beer & Cider Festival, Hackney, London

6 Wednesday
Pigs Ear Beer & Cider Festival, Hackney, London

10 Sunday ◑

7 Thursday
Pigs Ear Beer & Cider Festival, Hackney, London

Monday		4	11	18	25
Tuesday		5	12	19	26
Wednesday		6	13	20	27
Thursday		7	14	21	28
Friday	1	8	15	22	29
Saturday	2	9	16	23	30
Sunday	3	10	17	24	31

Hogs Back TEA (4.2%)

Hogs Back Brewery, Tongham, Surrey

hogsback.co.uk

16th December – Boston Tea Party, 1773

'No taxation without representation,' was a rallying cry heard among New England colonists. On the evening of 16 December 1773, their grievance came to a head. Angered by favouritism being shown by British Parliament to the East India Company by the introduction of the Tea Act, which allowed it to transport tea to America tax-free, thus undercutting local merchants, citizens of Boston blockaded three of the company's ships and demanded that they leave the harbour without unloading their cargo. But the British Governor refused to let the vessels sail until the locals had paid duty on the tea. With stalemate achieved, it was time for drastic action. On the night of 16 December, a group of patriots launched an attack on the ships. Around 150 men stole aboard and hacked apart 342 tea chests, depositing the contents into the water. The Boston Tea Party, as it became known, proved to be one of the catalysts for the forthcoming War of Independence.

As part of the growing protest against the British, the American colonists boycotted the drinking of tea. No doubt they found an able replacement in beer. In the UK, you can now enjoy both at the same time, thanks to a brew called TEA from Hogs Back Brewery in Surrey. The letters apparently stand for Traditional English Ale and that's exactly what it is – tea-brown in colour and admirably balancing the nutty flavours of pale and crystal malt with the smoky orange fruitiness of Fuggle and, particularly, Golding hops. It's as British a beer as you're likely to find – and the Americans appreciate it, too.

The Boston Tea Party

11 Monday

15 Friday

12 Tuesday

16 Saturday

13 Wednesday

First day of Hanukkah

17 Sunday

14 Thursday

Monday		4	11	18	25
Tuesday		5	12	19	26
Wednesday		6	13	20	27
Thursday		7	14	21	28
Friday	1	8	15	22	29
Saturday	2	9	16	23	30
Sunday	3	10	17	24	31

De Dolle Brouwers Stille Nacht (12%)

De Dolle Brouwers, Esen

dedollebrouwers.be

24th December – Christmas truce in the trenches, 1914

If ever there was a perfect counterpoint to the madness of war, Christmas Eve 1914 provided it. World War I had started in earnest in August of that year. By December, thousands of lives had already been lost, and for the soldiers on both sides of the front line, life was bleak.

As darkness fell on 24 December, the mood changed dramatically. The Germans had been sent small Christmas trees and candles. They decided to share them with their adversaries, raising them above the trenches. At first the Allies were bemused, even more so when the enemy began singing a song whose words they couldn't understand but whose tune was all too familiar. The carol was 'Stille Nacht' ('Silent Night'). Soon, some brave German souls climbed out of their hiding places. The Allies reciprocated. Hands were shaken, sentiments were exchanged about the misery of the war, and small tokens of friendship passed between them as the spirit of Christmas descended onto the battlefield.

The beer selected for today is strong enough to send the drinker into a reflective mood, and a little thought about the sacrifices made by those engaged in that brutal war is not inappropriate at this time of plenty. It is brewed by De Dolle Brouwers near Diksmuide, Flanders, close to the scene of the carnage, and it goes by the name of Stille Nacht.

Stille Nacht is a sublime example of the brewers' art, constructed from pale malt and candy sugar, and laced with Nugget hops from the nearby hop gardens at Poperinge. Golden and naturally effervescent, it presents a spicy, smoothly malty aroma that is packed with the zest of oranges. The same crisp, citrus notes take the lead in the taste, which is nicely warming, and the body is surprisingly light for the strength. The bittersweet, drying, almost burning finish marks this out as a beer with huge character and yet one that is not too demanding. There can be few better ways in which to slip reverently into a Christmas frame of mind.

18 Monday ●

19 Tuesday

20 Wednesday
Last day of Hanukkah

21 Thursday
Winter solstice

22 Friday

23 Saturday

24 Sunday
Christmas Eve

Monday		4	11	18	25
Tuesday		5	12	19	26
Wednesday		6	13	20	27
Thursday		7	14	21	28
Friday	1	8	15	22	29
Saturday	2	9	16	23	30
Sunday	3	10	17	24	31

St-Sylvestre 3 Monts (8.5%)

Brasserie de St-Sylvestre, St-Sylvestre-Cappel

brasserie-st-sylvestre.com

Frescoes in the oratory of St Sylvester, Rome

31st December – St Sylvester's Day

It's the last day of the year and we all want something a little bit special with which to see in the next 12 months. St-Sylvestre 3 Monts is not just a fine beer, it also has a significance in that it is brewed in a village named after the saint whose feast day falls on 31 December. St Sylvester was born in Rome, probably in the late third century. He rose through the ranks of early Christians to the point where, on the death of Pope Miltiades, he was selected as his successor. It was during Sylvester's 21-year papacy that the Emperor Constantine converted to Christianity, thereby turning an erstwhile persecuted religion into an accepted faith.

St-Sylvestre-Cappel is located just south of Dunkirk, in Flanders hop-growing country close to the Belgian border, and is best known today for its brewery. St-Sylvestre 3 Monts – named after three small hills close to the village – was introduced in 1985. It's a pale golden ale in the bière de garde tradition, which means that it is matured at the brewery before being filtered for the bottle. It is a surprisingly delicate beer, extremely easy to drink for its strength. Smooth, sweet pale malt, a fruity acidic zing and a perfumed, spicy warmth are the main features, with a drying, spicy, delicately hoppy finish to round off.

3 Monts is presented in a tall corked bottle. The label describes the beer as *'Bière Spéciale Dégustation'* – a special beer to savour – and proffers the friendly advice, *'A consommer avec modération'* – in other words, take it easy. On New Year's Eve, that may prove difficult, but you've been warned!

25 Monday

Christmas Day
Public holiday UK

26 Tuesday ◐

Boxing Day
Public holiday UK

27 Wednesday

28 Thursday

29 Friday

30 Saturday

31 Sunday

New Year's Eve

Monday		4	11	18	25
Tuesday		5	12	19	26
Wednesday		6	13	20	27
Thursday		7	14	21	28
Friday	1	8	15	22	29
Saturday	2	9	16	23	30
Sunday	3	10	17	24	31

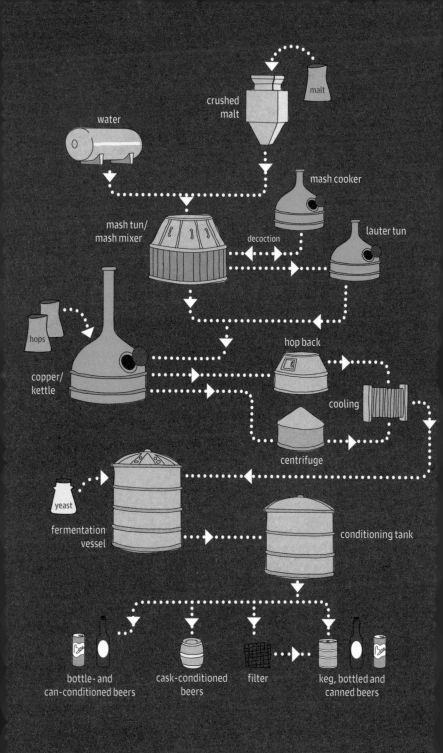

malt

crushed malt

water

mash cooker

mash tun/
mash mixer

decoction

lauter tun

hops

copper/
kettle

hop back

cooling

centrifuge

yeast

fermentation
vessel

conditioning tank

bottle- and
can-conditioned beers

cask-conditioned
beers

filter

keg, bottled and
canned beers

How beer is brewed

Beer is made from just four key ingredients: barley, water, hops and yeast. Brewers use other ingredients for flavour, or according to local traditions, but at its simplest beer can be created from the sugary extract obtained from steeping malted barley in hot water, with hops for flavour and yeast to convert the sugars into alcohol and carbon dioxide.

Barley

Barley is beer's building block. Other grain can be used and many brewers blend in small amounts of wheat or oats and even rye, but barley is the preferred grain because it works in perfect harmony with hops and yeast.

But barley has to be turned into malt before it can be used in brewing. Maltsters steep barley in water to absorb moisture, then spread it on heated floors or inside rotating drums where it starts to germinate. Once germination is under way, the grain is transferred to an oven known as a kiln. Heat dries the grain and, depending on the temperature, produces pale or darker malts.

Pale malt is the main ingredient in beer as it has the highest level of enzymes – natural chemical catalysts – that are crucial to the brewing process. Brown, black and chocolate malts are used for colour and flavour in darker beers. Depending on the mix of malts, the grain will give aromas and flavours similar to Horlicks, Ovaltine, oatmeal biscuits, Ryvita, almonds and other nuts, honey, butterscotch, caramel, tobacco and vanilla.

Water

When malt reaches the brewery, it's ground in a mill into a powder called grist. Grist and pure hot water, called 'liquor' by brewers, flow into the mash tun, where the porridge-like mixture of grain and water starts the brewing process. Pure water can come from springs, bore holes or from the public supply. It will be thoroughly filtered, and brewers often add such sulphates as gypsum and magnesium to enhance the flavours of malt and hops. The mixture is left to stand in the mash tun for some two hours and during that time enzymes in the malt convert the remaining starch into fermentable sugar.

When starch conversion is complete, the brewer and his team will run the sweet extract, called wort, to a second vessel, the copper, where it's vigorously boiled with hops. The hops are usually added in stages: at the start of the boil, half way through and just before the end, in order to extract the maximum aroma and bitterness from the plants.

Hops

There are around two dozen hop varieties in England, ranging from the Golding and the Fuggle, first grown in the 18th and 19th centuries, to more modern ones, such as Boadicea and Endeavour. Hops can be used in the brewery either as whole flowers or ground and compressed into pellets. Hops grow at great speed in the spring and summer and once harvested they are dried by warm air in special sheds or oast houses. Hops contain acids, oils and resins that deliver bitterness to beer along with fragrant aromas of spice, pepper, grass, cedar wood and citrus fruit. The oils and tannins in the plant help stabilise beer and prevent infection. English hops are prized for their spice and pepper notes, but other varieties give the aromas and flavours of grapefruit, mango and tropical fruits demanded by many modern brewers.

The copper boil lasts between 1½ and 2 hours. The hopped wort is passed through a cooler to lower the temperature and is then pumped to fermenting vessels. These can be open or closed, upright or horizontal, but it's here that the liquid starts the conversion to alcohol with the aid of yeast. Yeast is a fungus that feeds on sugary liquids. Every brewery has its own yeast culture that gives an important 'house' character to the beer.

Fermentation

Ale fermentation is rapid and lasts for a week – it's a method known as 'warm fermentation' to distinguish it from the cold fermentation method used to make genuine lager. Yeast converts malt sugar into alcohol and carbon dioxide and creates a dense, rocky blanket on top of the liquid. It also produces natural chemical compounds called esters that give off aromas reminiscent of apples, oranges, pear drops, banana, liquorice, molasses and, in especially strong beers, fresh leather. These add to the complexity of the finished beer.

Eventually the yeast will be overcome by the alcohol it has created and the yeast blanket is skimmed from the vessel. The beer will rest for several days in conditioning tanks to mature and to purge unwanted rough alcohols and esters.

Dispense

The next stage of the process depends on how the beer will be packaged and sold. In the UK the majority of ales are sold in cask-conditioned form. Cask ale is not finished in the brewery but in the pub cellar. From conditioning tanks, it's racked into casks. Finings are added to clear the beer. Additional hops may be placed in the casks for extra aroma and flavour and brewing sugar can be added to encourage a strong secondary fermentation. As the beer sits in the pub cellar, the remaining yeast turns the final sugars into alcohol and carbon dioxide – this carbonation gives the beer what is known as 'condition'.

Similarly beer can be bottle- or can-conditioned, with beer being racked into bottles or cans containing a small amount of live yeast to ensure natural carbonation.

The alternative to cask-conditioned beer is brewery-conditioned beer. This beer does not contain live yeast and is filtered and pasteurized. It is then artificially carbonated and packaged in a pressurized keg and served under additional pressure from carbon dioxide.

Beer's four main ingredients

Hops: There are around two dozen hop varieties in England, ranging from the Golding and the Fuggle, first grown in the 18th and 19th centuries, to more modern ones, such as Boadicea and Endeavour. Hops can be used in the brewery either as whole flowers or ground and compressed into pellets.

Water: Pure water, called 'liquor' by brewers, can come from springs, bore holes or from the public supply. It will be thoroughly filtered, and brewers often add such sulphates as gypsum and magnesium to enhance the flavours of malt and hops.

Malt: Maltsters steep barley in water to absorb moisture, then spread it on heated floors or inside rotating drums where it starts to germinate. Once germination is under way, the grain is transferred to an oven known as a kiln. Heat dries the grain and, depending on the temperature, produces pale or darker malts.

Yeast: Yeast is a type of fungus that feeds on sugary liquids. Every brewery will have its own yeast culture that's carefully guarded and stored, as it gives its own important 'house' character to the beer. Brewers keep samples of their yeast cultures in a special bank in Norwich in case they need a fresh supply.

Beer styles

British beer used to be defined by just a handful of styles. Happily for drinkers, the choice is now never-ending: brewers both in the UK and overseas are experimenting with and recreating hundreds of different styles, whilst the range of foreign beers available to British drinkers has never been greater. Here is a guide to some of the most commonly-available British and Continental styles.

Porter and stout

Porter was a London beer that created the first commercial brewing industry in the world in the early 18th century. Its name came from its popularity with London porters. The strongest version of porter was called stout porter, later shortened to just stout.

During World War One, when the British government stopped brewers from using heavily roasted malts in order to divert energy to the arms industry, Guinness and other Irish brewers came to dominate the market.

Look for a jet-black colour and expect a dark and roasted grain character with burnt fruit, espresso or cappuccino coffee, liquorice and molasses. The beer should have a deep bitterness to balance the richness of malt and fruit.

Mild

Mild developed in the 18th and 19th centuries as drinkers started to demand a slightly sweeter and less aggressively hopped beer than Porter. Mild ale was drunk primarily by industrial and agricultural workers, who needed to refresh themselves after long hours of arduous labour. Early milds were much stronger than modern versions, which tend to fall into the 3–3.5% category. Mild is usually dark brown in colour, owing to the use of well-roasted malts or roasted barley. Look for a rich malty aroma and flavour, with hints of dark fruit, chocolate, coffee and caramel, with a gentle underpinning of hop bitterness.

Old ale

Old ale is another style from the 18th century, stored for many months or even years in wooden vessels where the beer picked up some lactic sourness from wild yeasts and tannins in the wood. As a result of the sour taste, it was dubbed 'stale' by drinkers. Contrary to expectations, old ales do not have to be especially strong and can be no more than 4% alcohol. Neither do they have to be dark: old ale can be pale and bursting with lush malt, tart fruit and spicy hops. Darker versions will have a more profound malt character, with powerful hints of roasted grain, dark fruit, polished leather and fresh tobacco. The hallmark of the style is a lengthy period of maturation, often in bottle rather than cask.

Barley wine

Barley wine dates from the 18th and 19th centuries when England was often at war with France and it was the duty of patriots, usually from the upper classes, to drink ale rather than French claret. Barley wine had to be strong – often between 10% and 12% – and was stored for as long as 18 months or two years. Expect massive sweet malt and ripe fruit of the pear drop, mandarin orange and lemon type, with chocolate and coffee if darker malts are used. Hop rates are generous and produce bitterness and peppery, grassy and floral notes.

IPA

India pale ale changed the face of brewing in the 19th century. The new technologies of the Industrial Revolution enabled brewers to

Beer styles

use pale malts to design beers that were pale bronze in colour. 19th-century IPAs were high in both alcohol and hops to keep them in good condition during the journey to the colonies. Look for a big peppery hop aroma and palate balanced by juicy malt and tart citrus fruit.

Pale ale

Pale ales were a version of IPA brewed for the domestic market. From the early 20th century, Bitter began to overtake Pale Ale in popularity and as a result pale ale became mainly a bottled product. A true pale ale should be different to bitter, similar in colour and style to IPA and brewed without the addition of coloured malts. It should have a spicy/resinous aroma and palate with biscuit malt and tart fruit from the hops. Many beers called bitter today should properly be labelled pale ale.

Bitter

At the turn of the 19th and 20th centuries, brewers built large estates of 'tied' pubs and they moved away from beers stored for months or years and developed 'running beers' that could be served after a few days of conditioning in pub cellars. Bitter was a new type of running beer: it developed from pale ale but was usually copper coloured or deep bronze owing to the use of slightly darker malts, such as crystal, that gave the beer fullness of palate. Best is a stronger version of bitter. With ordinary bitter, look for spicy, peppery and grassy hop character, a powerful bitterness, tangy fruit and juicy/nutty malt. With best and strong bitters, malt and fruit character will tend to dominate but hop aroma and bitterness are still crucial to the style, often achieved by 'late hopping' during the copper boil or by adding additional hops to casks as they leave the brewery.

Burton ale

As the name suggests, the origins of Burton Ale lie in Burton-on-Trent, but the style became so popular in the 18th and 19th centuries that most brewers had 'a Burton' in their portfolio and the expression 'gone for a Burton' entered the English language. Bass in Burton at one time had six different versions of the beer,

ranging from 6% to 11.5%: the strongest versions were exported to Russia and the Baltic States. In the 20th century, Burton was overtaken in popularity by Pale Ale and Bitter but it was revived with great success in the late 1970s with the launch of Ind Coope Draught Burton Ale. Look for a bright amber colour, a rich malt and fruit character underscored by a solid resinous and cedar wood hop note.

Golden ale

Golden ales were first brewed in the early 1980s to target younger drinkers of mass-produced lager and introduce them to the pleasures of cask ale. Golden ale is often brewed with lager malt or specially-produced low-colour ale malt and, as a result, hops are allowed to give full expression, balancing sappy malt with luscious fruit, floral, herbal, spicy and resinous notes. They are often served colder than draught bitter.

Wheat beer

Wheat beer is a style closely associated with Bavaria and Belgium and its popularity in Britain has encouraged many brewers to add wheat beers to their portfolios. The title is something of a misnomer as all 'wheat beers' are a blend of malted barley and wheat, as the latter grain is difficult to brew with and needs the addition of barley, which acts as a natural filter during the mashing stage. But wheat, if used with special yeast cultures developed for brewing the style, gives distinctive aromas and flavours, such as clove, banana and bubblegum, that make it a complex and refreshing beer. The Belgian version of wheat beer often has the addition of herbs and spices, such as milled coriander seeds and orange peel – a habit that dates back to medieval times.

Fruit/speciality beers

Brewers endlessly search for new flavours to reach out to a wider audience for their beers. The popularity in Britain of Belgian fruit beers has not gone unoticed and now many domestic brewers are using fruit in their beer. Others add honey, herbs, heather, spice and even spirits – brandy and rum feature in a number of speciality beers, while other beers are matured in Bourbon, whisky and Cognac casks. The ingredients add new dimensions to the brewing process and are highly fermentable, with the result that beers that use the likes of cherries or raspberries are dry and quenching rather than cloying.

Scottish beers

Historically, Scottish beers tend to be darker and maltier than beers south of the border, the reflection of a colder climate where beer needs to be nourishing. The classic traditional styles are Light, Heavy and Export, which are not dissimilar to mild, bitter and IPA. They are also known as 60, 70 and 80 Shilling ales from a 19th-century system of invoicing beers according to strength. A 'Wee Heavy' or 90 Shilling ale, now rare, is the Scottish equivalent of barley wine. Many of the newer brewers in Scotland are producing beers lighter in colour and with pronounced hop character.

Pilsner

Pilsner was originally a golden, hoppy lager brewed in the city of Pilsen in Bohemia, now part of the Czech Republic. A true Pilsner is usually around 4.5–5% ABV. In Germany, many brewers either spell the word Pilsener or shorten it to Pils, to avoid any suggestion their beers come from Pilsen. In the Czech Republic, Pilsner is an 'appellation': only beers from Pilsen can use the term.

Kölsch

Kölsch is a golden ale brewed in Cologne and protected by a special ordinance. It was first brewed as a response to the growing popularity of Pilsner. Kölsch uses ale yeast but undergoes a period of cold conditioning. It is a delicate beer with a soft fruity flavour.

Trappist/Abbey beers

Trappist beers are part of the ale family and are made in breweries in Belgium, the Netherlands and France controlled by Trappist monks. Trappist beers carry the 'Authentic Trappist Product' logo that differentiates them from commercially-brewed beers, which are known as Abbey beers. These beers are produced principally in Belgium and may be brewed under licence from monasteries, though some have no monastic links whatsoever. Abbey beers are labelled Abbaye (French) or Abdij (Flemish).

Bock

Bock is a German term for a strong beer, which can be pale or dark, usually stored or lagered for several months. The term is associated with the 'liquid bread' beers brewed by monks to sustain them during Lent. In the Netherlands, the term is sometimes spelt Bok, and beers there may be warm fermented.

Bière de garde

French 'keeping beer', a style mostly associated with French Flanders and first brewed by farmer/brewers in spring and stored to refresh their labourers during the summer months. It is now produced all year round.

Saison

Saison is another Belgian beer style growing in popularity. It originates in Wallonia, the French-speaking region of Belgium, and was a seasonal beer brewed by farmers to refresh their labourers during the busy harvest period. In sharp contrast to lambic, Saison should have a rich malty/fruity palate balanced by earthy, spicy and peppery hops. Some Saisons are made with the addition of 'botanicals' such as ginger, black pepper and aniseed.

Lambic and Sour beers

Lambic beer is made by 'wild' or spontaneous fermentation. Rather than using carefully cultivated brewer's yeast, lambic is left open to the atmosphere to allow wild yeasts to attack the sugars in the wort and begin the fermentation. This process takes place in 'cool ships' (open cooling trays) that enable the wort to be attacked by passing yeasts such as *Brettanomyces*. Following the first fermentation, true lambics are stored in wooden casks for up to three years. The more recent style of Sour beer has been inspired by the lambic tradition. Instead of using open fermenters and airborne yeasts, most modern brewers inoculate their worts with '*Brett*' in order to gain the required sour or acidic character.

The bad beer guide

A poor pint of beer is something, unfortunately, we all encounter at some point.
But what, exactly, could be wrong with the beer?
To help, here's a simple checklist of common faults found in badly-kept real ale.

APPEARANCE	LIKELY CAUSE
Warm to the taste	Slow turnover; warm beer lines
Warm to the touch	Newly-washed glass
Flat and insipid – lacks character	Old cask
Hazy (but fresh taste – often apples or sulphur)	Fresh cask still to settle
Cloudy (often with undesirable tastes)	Yeast/bacteria in suspension; old cask
Unusual/undesirable tastes (sour, parsnip, celery, sweat)	Bacterial infection
Other unusual/undesirable tastes (TCP, sewers, wood, plastic, creosote)	Wild yeast infection

Rules for storing bottled beer

1 Always buy fresh stock
Some bottle-conditioned beers mature wonderfully in the bottle but most beer is undoubtedly best drunk young, so buy beers with plenty of time left before the 'best before' date.

2 Keep beers in a dark place
Light is an enemy of beer. If a beer is exposed to bright lights (sunlight or artificial), a chemical reaction can take place that leads to unpleasant flavours and 'skunky' aromas. For this reason, also be wary of beers packaged in clear or green bottles that are far less efficient than brown bottles in protecting beer from light.

3 Keep beers cool
As with all foodstuffs, low (but not freezing) temperatures help preserve beer. When it comes to serving the beer, check the temperature advice on the label.

4 Keep beers upright
This is not important with filtered beers but any beer that contains a sediment should be kept upright, or at least returned to the vertical well in advance of serving, to ensure the sediment remains at the bottom. For beers designed to be poured cloudy, this is not such an issue. Also beers in corked bottles need to be stored horizontally (to keep the cork moist and tight), but then returned to the upright well before serving.

'Beer', 'brewery' and 'cheers!' in other languages

LANGUAGE	BEER	BREWERY	CHEERS!
Bulgarian	bira	pivovarna	na zdrave!
Chinese	pi jiu	niang jiu chang	gan bei!
Croatian	pivo	pivovara	živjeli!
Czech	pivo	pivovar	na zdraví!
Danish	øl	bryggeri	skål!
Dutch	bier	brouwerij	proost!
Esperanto	biero	bierfarejo	je via sano!
Estonian	õlu	õllevabrik	terviseks!
Finnish	olut	olutpanimo	kippis!
French	bière	brasserie	santé!
Gaelic	beoir	grúdlann	sláinte!
German	bier	brauerei	prost!
Greek	bira	zythopoieío	yamas!
Hungarian	sör	sörfozde	egészségére!
Italian	birra	birreria	salute/cin cin!
Japanese	biiru	jouzousho	kanpai!
Latvian	alus	alus daritava	priekā!
Lithuanian	alus	alaus darykla	buk sveikas!
Norwegian	øl	bryggeri	skål!
Polish	piwo	browar	na zdrowie!
Portuguese	cerveja	cervejaria	saúde!
Romanian	bere	berar	noroc!
Russian	pivo	pivovarennyjzavod	na zdorovie!
Spanish	cerveza	cervecería	salud!
Swedish	öl	bryggeri	skål!
Welsh	cwrw	bragdy	iechyd da!

The European Beer Consumers Union (EBCU)

The European Beer Consumers Union (EBCU) was formed in Bruges in 1990 by three founding beer consumer organisations, representing Belgium, the Netherlands and the United Kingdom. They have since been joined by similarly-minded national consumer groups from Austria, the Czech Republic, Denmark, Finland, Ireland, Italy, Norway, Poland, Sweden and Switzerland.

The EBCU acts as the voice of the European beer consumer to the European Parliament and Commission and to the European beer industry. It is totally independent from breweries or other vested interests, as are all its member organisations, and campaigns for four aims and objectives:

- Preservation of European Beer Culture
- Promotion of Traditional Beers
- Support of Traditional Breweries
- Representation of Beer Drinkers

ITS MEMBER ORGANISATIONS ARE:

AUSTRIA
BierIG Österreich
info@bierig.org
www.bierig.org

BELGIUM
Zythos
rvb@zythos.be
www.zythos.be

CZECH REPUBLIC
Sdružení přátel piva
erlich@pratelepiva.cz
www.pratelepiva.cz

DENMARK
Danske Ølentusiaster
anne.lise.knoerr@ale.dk
www.ale.dk

FINLAND
Olutliitto
andre.brunnsberg@gmail.com
www.olutliitto.fi

IRELAND
Beoir
admin@beoir.org
www.beoir.org

ITALY
Unionbirrai
info@unionbirrai.com
www.unionbirrai.com

NETHERLANDS
PINT (Vereniging Promotie INformatie Traditioneel Bier)
info@pint.nl
www.pint.nl

NORWAY
NORØL (Norske Ølvenners Landsforbund)
post@nor-ale.org
www.nor-ale.org

POLAND
Bractwo Piwne
ebcu@bractwopiwne.pl
www.bractwopiwne.pl

SWEDEN
Svenska Ölfrämjandet
info@svenskaolframjandet.org
www.svenskaolframjandet.se

SWITZERLAND
ABO (L'Association des Buveurs d'Orge)
info@abo-ch.org
www.abo-ch.org

UNITED KINGDOM
CAMRA (Campaign for Real Ale)
camra@camra.org.uk
www.camra.org.uk

Glossary

ABV (Alcohol by Volume): international method for measuring and declaring for tax purposes the strength of beer.

Adjuncts: cereals and sugars added to beer, often as a cheap substitute, but sometimes used by brewers for special flavours. Adjuncts are not permitted in Germany where the *Reinheitsgebot* allows only malted grain.

Ale: the world's oldest beer type, produced by warm or top fermentation. The term covers such styles as mild, bitter, porter, stout, old ale, barley wine, Abbey and Trappist ales, and some types of Bock.

Alpha acid: the natural acid in the cone of the hop plant that gives bitterness to beer.

Aroma: the 'nose' of a beer that gives an indication of the malty, hoppy and possibly fruity characteristics to be found in the mouth.

Barley: the preferred grain used by all brewers as the main ingredient in beer and source of fermentable sugar.

Beer: generic term for an alcoholic drink made from grain. It includes ale, lager and Belgian lambic/gueuze.

Bottle conditioned/bottle fermented: a beer bottled with live yeast that allows the beer to mature, gain condition ('sparkle') and extra alcohol in its glass container.

Brewpub: a pub that brews beer on the premises.

Campaign for Real Ale (CAMRA): beer drinkers' organisation founded in 1971 to protect cask-conditioned beer – dubbed 'real ale'.

Carbon dioxide (CO_2): a gas naturally produced by fermentation. In cask-conditioned ale or bottle-conditioned beer, the gas is natural. When beers are filtered in the brewery, CO_2 may added either in the brewery or as part of the dispense system in a bar or pub.

Cask ale: also known as cask beer or real ale. A draught beer that undergoes a secondary fermentation in the cask in the pub cellar, reaching maturity as a result of natural processes. The style is mainly confined to Britain.

Condition: the level of carbon dioxide (CO_2) present in beer, which gives beer its sparkle.

Copper: vessel used to boil the sugary wort with hops. Traditionally made of copper but more often today of stainless steel.

Dunkel: German for 'dark', indicating a lager beer in which colour is derived from well-roasted malts.

EBC: European Brewing Convention. A scale that measures the colour of a finished beer. A Pilsner may have 6–8 units, an English pale ale 20–40, porters and stouts 150–300 or more.

Esters: Flavour compounds produced by the action of yeast turning sugars into alcohol and carbon dioxide (CO_2). Esters are often similar to fruits, and fruitiness is associated with members of the ale family.

Fermentation: turning malt sugars into alcohol and carbon dioxide (CO_2) by the action of yeast. Ale is made by warm fermentation, lager by cold fermentation.

Fining: clarifying beer with the addition of finings, usually isinglass made from fish bladders. Caragheen [Irish Moss] can also be used and is preferred by vegetarians and vegans.

Finish: the aftertaste of a beer; the impression left at the back of the tongue and the throat.

Grist: brewers' term for the milled grains to be used in a brew. The term comes from the word 'grind' and is still used in the expression 'all grist to the mill'.

Hefe: German for yeast. Beers 'mit hefe' are naturally conditioned and not filtered. Usually applies to wheat beers.

Glossary

Helles: German for light, indicating a pale beer, either lager or wheat beer.

Hops: climbing plant with cones containing acids, resins and tannins that gives aroma and bitterness to beer, and helps prevent bacterial infection.

IBUs (also known as EBUs): International or European Units of Bitterness. A measure of the acids in hops that create bitterness in beer. Some extremely bland international lagers have around 10–15 IBUs whereas a pale ale or IPA will start at around 40 and can rise as high as 75 or 80.

IPA: short for India Pale Ale. First brewed for soldiers and civil servants based in India.

Lager: from the German meaning store or storage place. The world's most popular beer type, produced by cool or bottom fermentation. Following primary fermentation, beer is 'cold conditioned' in tanks, during which a slow secondary fermentation takes place, carbonation increases, and a clean, quenching, spritzy beer results.

Liquor: brewers' term for the pure water used in the mashing and boiling process.

Malt: grain – usually barley – that has been partially germinated, dried and cured or toasted in a kiln. The colour of malt is determined by the degree of heat in the kiln. All beers are made primarily from pale malt, colour and flavour are derived from darker malts.

Mash: the mixture of malted grain and pure hot water, the first stage of the brewing process, when sugars are extracted from the malt.

Mash tun: vessel in which malted grain is mixed with 'liquor' to start the brewing process.

Micro-brewery: a small brewery with a small staff, often just a couple of people, brewing batches of beer for local distribution.

Mouthfeel: the sensation that beer and its constituent parts – malt, hops and fruity esters – make in the mouth.

Original Gravity (OG): system once used in Britain for measuring the level of 'fermentable material' – malt, other grains and sugars – in a beer.

Pasteurisation: heating process developed by Louis Pasteur that kills bacteria and stabilises the beer. If pasteurisation is clumsy, the beer can take on unpleasant aromas and flavours.

Porter: a brown (later black) beer first brewed in London early in the 18th century. The strongest porters were known as stout.

Real ale: term coined by CAMRA in Britain to denote a beer that is neither filtered nor pasteurised, which undergoes a secondary fermentation in its container and is not served by applied gas pressure.

Reinheitsgebot: the Bavarian 'Pure Beer Law' dating from 1516 that lays down that only malted barley and/or wheat, hops, yeast and water can be used in brewing.

Sparge: to rinse the grain after mashing to flush out any remaining malt sugars (from the French *esperger*, meaning to sprinkle).

Wort: the sweet, sugary extract produced by mashing malt and water. Wort is boiled with hops, then cooled prior to fermentation.

Yeast: a natural fungus that attacks sweet liquids such as wort, turning malt sugars into alcohol and carbon dioxide (CO_2). Brewers' yeasts are either warm or top fermenting cultures for ale brewing, or cold or bottom fermenting cultures for lager brewing. Belgian lambic brewers use wild yeasts from the atmosphere.

Index of beers

Beers tried in 2017

Beers tried in 2017

Beers tried in 2017

Beers tried in 2017

Pubs visited in 2017

Pubs visited in 2017

Pubs visited in 2017

Pubs visited in 2017

Notes

Notes

Notes

Notes

Books for beer lovers

CAMRA Books, the publishing arm of the Campaign for Real Ale, is the leading publisher of books on beer and pubs. Key titles include:

Good Beer Guide 2017

Editor: **ROGER PROTZ**

CAMRA's *Good Beer Guide* is fully revised and updated each year and features pubs across the United Kingdom that serve the best real ale. Now in its 44th edition, this pub guide is completely independent with listings based entirely on nomination and evaluation by CAMRA members. This means you can be sure that every one of the 4,500 pubs deserves their place, plus they all come recommended by people who know a thing or two about good beer.

£15.99   ISBN 978-1-85249-335-6

So You Want to Be a Beer Expert?

JEFF EVANS

More people than ever are searching for an understanding of what makes a great beer, and this book meets that demand by presenting a hands-on course in beer appreciation, with sections on understanding the beer styles of the world, beer flavours, how beer is made, the ingredients, and more. Uniquely, *So You Want to Be a Beer Expert?* doesn't just relate the facts, but helps readers reach conclusions for themselves. Key to this are the interactive tastings that show readers, through their own taste-buds, what beer is all about. CAMRA's *So You Want to Be a Beer Expert?* is the ideal book, for anyone who wants to further their knowledge and enjoyment of beer.

£12.99   ISBN 978-1-85249-322-6

Yorkshire Pub Walks

BOB STEEL

CAMRA's *Yorkshire Pub Walks* guides you round the best of England's largest county, while never straying too far from a decent pint. A practical, pocket-sized guide to some of the best pubs and best walking in Yorkshire, this fully illustrated book features 25 walks around some of Yorkshire's most awe-inspiring National Parks and landscapes, and its most vibrant towns and cities. Full-colour Ordnance Survey maps and detailed route information, plus pub listings with opening hours and details of draught beers, make CAMRA's *Yorkshire Pub Walks* the essential guide for anyone wanting a taste of 'God's Own County'.

£9.99   ISBN 978-1-85249-329-5

CAMRA's Beer Anthology

Editor: **ROGER PROTZ**

Beer is deeply engrained in the culture and history of the British Isles. From the earliest times, the pleasures of ale and beer have been recorded for posterity. Shakespeare, Dickens and Hardy all wrote on the delights of beer and pubs. They are joined today by a small army of writers with a different aim: they are not commenting on beer in passing, as part of a literary endeavour, but are dedicated full time to researching, promoting and championing beer. From bards to biographers to beer bloggers, explore the world of beer as seen through the eyes of writers as diverse as Bill Bryson, William Blake, Douglas Adams, Melissa Cole, Dylan Thomas, Breandán Kearney, James Joyce, Thomas Hardy, Jeff Evans and George Orwell.

£9.99   ISBN 978-1-85249-333-2

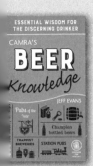

CAMRA's Beer Knowledge

JEFF EVANS

A fully revised and updated collection of conversation-starting anecdotes, useful pub facts and figures, and trivia, *CAMRA's Beer Knowledge* is the perfect gift for any beer lover. More than 200 entries cover the serious, the silly and the downright bizarre from the world of beer. Inside this pint-sized compendium you'll find everything from the biggest brewer in the world to the beers with the daftest names. A quick skim before a night out and you'll always have enough beery wisdom to impress your friends. Meticulously researched by award-winning beer writer Jeff Evans, *CAMRA's Beer Knowledge* is the beer book that everyone should own.

£9.99   ISBN 978-1-85249-338-7

Britain's Best Real Heritage Pubs

GEOFF BRANDWOOD

Britain's Best Real Heritage Pubs is the result of 25 years' research by CAMRA to discover pubs that are either unaltered in 70 years or have features of truly national historic importance. Among the 260 pubs, there are unspoilt country locals, Victorian drinking palaces and mighty roadhouses. The book has features describing how the pub developed, what's distinctive about pubs in different parts of the country, how people a century ago could expect to be served drinks at their table, and how they used the pub for take-out sales in the pre-supermarket era.

£9.99   ISBN 978-1-85249-334-9

der these and other CAMRA books online at **www.camra.org.uk/books**,
k at your local bookstore, or contact: CAMRA, 230 Hatfield Road, St Albans, AL1 4LW.
lephone 01727 867201

A campaign of two halves

Campaigning for pub goers and beer drinkers

CAMRA, the Campaign for Real Ale, is the not-for-profit independent voice of
real ale drinkers and pub goers. CAMRA's vision is to have quality real ale
and thriving pubs in every community. We campaign tirelessly to achieve this goal,
as well as lobbying government to champion drinkers' rights. As a CAMRA member
you will have the opportunity to campaign to save pubs under threat of closure,
for pubs to be free to serve a range of real ales at fair prices and for a long-term
freeze in beer duty that will help Britain's brewing industry survive.

Enjoying real ale and pubs

CAMRA has over 175,000 members from all ages and backgrounds, brought
together by a common belief in the issues that CAMRA deals with and their love of
good quality British beer. From just £24 a year* – that's less than a pint a month –
you can join CAMRA and enjoy the following benefits:

Subscription to *What's Brewing*, our monthly colour newspaper,
and *Beer*, our quarterly magazine, informing you about beer and pub news
and detailing events and beer festivals around the country.

Free or reduced entry to over 160 national, regional and local beer festivals.

Money off many of our publications including the *Good Beer Guide*,
the *Good Bottled Beer Guide* and *So You Want to Be a Beer Expert?*

Access to a members-only section of our website, **www.camra.org.uk**,
which gives up-to-the-minute news stories and includes a
special offer section with regular features.

Special discounts with numerous partner organisations and money off real ale
in your participating local pubs as part of our Pubs Discount Scheme.

Log onto **www.camra.org.uk/join** for CAMRA membership information.

CAMPAIGN
FOR
REAL ALE

*£24 membership cost stated is only available via Direct Debit, other concessionary rates available.
Please note membership rates stated are correct at the time of printing but are subject to change.
Full details of all membership rates can be found here: **www.camra.org.uk/membershiprates**